Light Works

Explorations In Art, Culture, And Creativity

Milenko Matanović

P · R · E · S · S

Issaquah, Washington
1985

Library of Congress Catalog Card #85-82035
ISBN 0-936878-11-8

Excerpts from Madeleine L'Engle's book, Walking on Water: Reflec-
tions on Faith and Art, by permission of Harold Shaw Publishers,
Copyright © Crosswicks, 1980.
Cover photo of James Hubbell's stained glass window by permis-
sion of photographer Otto B. Rigan from his book The Doors of
Abú Dhabi.
Cover design and caligraphy by David Verwolf.
Produced and edited by Suzanne Duroux.

First Edition, November, 1985.
Printed in the United States of America by Intercollegiate Press.

CONTENTS

ACKNOWLEDGMENTS   1

INTRODUCTION   3

SUZI GABLIK   7

JAMES HUBBELL   15

MATTHEW FOX   27

NAJ WIKOFF   39

WILLIAM IRWIN THOMPSON   49

PHILIP GLASS   63

SIR GEORGE TREVELYAN   77

MADELEINE L'ENGLE   85

JAMES PARKS MORTON   97

PAUL WINTER   109

DANE RUDHYAR   121

JOHN TODD   131

JOSÉ ARGÜELLES   143

RICHARD CHAMBERLAIN   153

DAVID SPANGLER   165

ELLEN BURSTYN   177

MARKO POGAČNIK   187

MILENKO MATANOVIĆ   195

ACKNOWLEDGMENTS

My thanks and love to those who gave so much of themselves to be interviewed or to contribute an article to *LightWorks*, and to the following individuals in acknowledgment of the tremendous contribution each has made to this book:

Barbara Thomas for the initial impetus for my writing;
John Cutrer for being such an angel;
David and Nancy Warner for the Apple II;
Grant Abert, Nancy Ward, and Margaret Lloyd for their sustaining friendship and financial assistance;
Marilyn Unruh for selecting excerpts from Madeleine L'Engle's book;
Otto Rigan for the use of his photos;
David Verwolf for much more than our contract outlined;
Rebecca Piep, Rue Hass, Rachel Roccamora, Paul Doremus, Kathi Lightstone Matanović, Dorothy Maclean, Katherine Collis, and David Spangler for transcribing, proofreading, and making numerous helpful suggestions;
and Suzanne Duroux, Editor and Production Coordinator, who very nearly put the book together herself, and without whose initiative and commitment *LightWorks* would still be only an idea.

INTRODUCTION

At the heart of every age is a unique impulse out of which, through the course of events and under favorable conditions, emerges a new cultural body. It is as if each age had its own "DNA," which lives first in the consciousness of only a few individuals who, like artists, ". . . create out of their irrational imaginations the planetary mystical perceptions that begin as heresy and end up as heritage."[1] An artist crafts a stained glass window by shaping pieces of colored glass into a pattern; but it is only when the light shines through that the work comes to life. In the same way, *LightWorks* brings together the perspectives of historians, philosophers, scientists, theologians, educators, and artists who are formulating compelling cultural possibilities. It was created with evolutionary light in mind, that cultural "DNA" which motivates the work of a growing number of individuals who share an awareness that at the core of any cultural change lie issues of creativity and artistry.

We have created a modern culture that is undeniably successful in establishing and promoting a consumer society, but in the process we have simultaneously caused a cancer in the social and environmental fabric. The debilitating fragmentation of Western culture—as reflected in pollution, deforestation, planned obsolescence, urban sprawl, and the threat of nuclear devastation—mirrors the darker side of human creativity. We simply ". . . increase the volume and the speed with which we move natural resources through the consumer economy to the junk pile or the waste heap,"[2] contaminating the air, soil, water, and human psyche. Some of our best schemes turn sour: in the pursuit of leisure, we create stress; in the quest for the solace and beauty of nature, away from the noise and pollution of our cities, we create sprawling suburbias and overcrowded parks, leaving little of the natural environment untouched. Good ideas and good intentions, in and of themselves, do not guarantee good results.

In order to insure integrity between our ideals and our actions, and between humanity and nature, we must gain a clearer understanding of the processes by which ideas and intentions take shape, or "incarnate." Perhaps the practice of artists can be our guide in this learning. The artistic sensibility consults and reflects upon divergent lifestyles and beliefs, upon intangible concepts and impressions, awakening our dormant potential and allowing new ideas and images to surface. If we accept the premise that future heritage can be detected in current artistic creations, then it is wise to consult artists, for they may offer invaluable guidelines for our next steps.

In my own explorations and consultations I have found the following aspects to represent some of the important elements of this practice:

* *Perceiving Connections.* Artistic work begins with silence. In the watching and listening which takes place in this silence, the world reveals its visible shapes and invisible mysteries to us. To perceive in an unobstructed fashion, free of expectations, undistorted by one's own projections, and liberated from the concensus reality is the first task of any artist. We are often motivated by decisions which are not intimately owned, decisions which are little more than the offspring of social convention and habit. If we want to identify our creations as our true progeny, we must have the courage to listen, observe, and trust our own perceptions. This inner communion serves as the essential foundation for our outer work. Forms created out of such an inner foundation enhance the harmony between ourselves and our world.

* *"Imagineering" the Future.* Through the skills of undistorted perception, the artist can become aware of the basic assumptions and guiding myths that govern the world. If these myths have outgrown their purpose—as indeed many of our current ones have—then the artist can take on the job of altering them, discarding the obsolete, empowering the appropriate, and creating the new. Artists, guided by their "owned" truths, can formulate these myths in their art works and disseminate them in their culture. Fred Polak, the Dutch futurist, stated that the rise and fall of images of the future precedes or accompanies the rise and fall of cultures. To engineer images of the future through the power of imagination, to have "imagineers," is essential to the health of all cultures, for a society's vitality is lost once its capacity to imagine is gone. The work of artists, in this view, represents culture's way of imagining beyond its linear and predictable patterns. Artists can be culture's scouts, forging paths into the future. Their works are, at their best, prophetic utterances.

* *Crafting Visions.* True art does not need to carry a message; it

must *be* the message. When art is crafted well, the message becomes invisible. There is an ever-present imperative for the artist to choose exactly the right words for the poem, precisely the right strokes, and colors, and lines for the painting, or the right stone to put into the wall. It must be just so, and there is no other way about it. When this imperative is carried into physical expression, the result is beautiful and simple. Like a river flowing through the land and seeking the path of least resistance, the artist can formulate equally uncomplicated solutions to complex problems. In a world where everything is becoming larger and more compounded, forms that are translucently simple offer true healing.

∗ *Liberating the Familiar.* In recycling, we take an old, discarded object with no apparent value and reidentify it by placing it into a new context. An artist is trained to look at objects from many angles, and like a child at play, uses those objects for numerous unorthodox purposes. In a culture where objects have been reduced to one-dimensional uses, this playful creativity is a magical rejuvenation that becomes an invaluable gift. Just as a gardener uses the compost of one season to stimulate the growth of the next, in the same way, the artist takes parts of the old disintegrating world and uses them as fertilizer for cultural change. Out of the chaos of the old, a new order—a new cosmos—is created.

∗ *Serving the Community.* Artists are custodians of beauty and aesthetic sensitivity, just as doctors are the custodians of health. In the face of nuclear war, artists need to come forward, offering their expertise to the process of creating peace and health on the planet. It is now an accepted notion that artists are individuals who have abdicated their social responsibility and are concerned only with their own work, accountable to no one but themselves, creating objects that become prisoners of museums, galleries, concert halls, theaters, and the homes of the wealthy. But art is meant to be free, and the sensitivity of artists is meant to be applied not only to their work, but to life at large. How can we create an artistic city, road, neighborhood, or organization or add an awareness of beauty and connectedness to the economic and political priorities? Imagine a city employing a Secretary of Beauty, whose job it is to review land-development projects. Or artists sitting on the boards of corporations and government bodies, stewarding the natural environment and helping to insure integrity and craftsmanship in all work.

∗ *"Arting" Oneself.* Alchemists of old sought to change lead into gold, symbolically transmuting the fragmented self and making it whole. The artist, like the alchemist, knows that the primary level of communication is with his or her own Being, and that art is only an extension of "beingness" into form. Also, by the laws of resonance, personal wholeness invokes wholeness in the world. Thus the first and greatest task is to "art" oneself, becoming a clearer channel through which to heal and uplift others.

*   *   *

Each of the interviews and articles in this book touches on some aspect(s) of these six themes. The explorations of the individuals included in *LightWorks* in art, culture, and creativity have consistently challenged and inspired my own inquiries. My hope is that their combined insight, experience, and example will be useful in illuminating new ideas, freeing imaginations, clarifying choices, and learning the "connective creativity" through which we can transform and heal ourselves. Then all our works become lightworks.

---

[1]From *Four Cultural Ecologies* by William Irwin Thompson; The Annals of Earth Stewardship, Vol I, Number 1, 1983.
[2]From *The Earth Community* by Thomas Berry; Teilhard Newsletter, Vol XIV, No. 2, 1981.

Suzi Gablik is an artist, art critic, writer, teacher, and lecturer currently living in London, England. She has been the London Correspondent for *Art in America*, the prestigious art news publication, since 1975. Her books include *Pop Art Redefined* (co-authored with John Russell), *Magritte, Progress in Art* and, most recently, *Has Modernism Failed?* She has lectured widely in universities and museums throughout the United States and Britain, as well as on international lecture tours sponsored by the United States International Communications Agency. She has also held the positions of Artist-in-Residence at Sydney College of the Arts, and Visiting Professor of Fine Arts at the University of the South in Tennessee.

I was reading Progress in Art *when I received a call from Suzi about the work I was doing through the ETA Project. It was clear that these issues had become a passionate concern for her, and I asked her to express that concern in an article for this book. I include it first because Suzi is able to see the need to change outmoded cultural paradigms from the perspective of the mainstream art world. She addresses the people in her field, calling artists to recognize that those who hold onto those paradigms are outpaced.*

*   *   *

Ever since modernism, the question "What is art for?" is one we don't like asking. Modernism taught us, perhaps all too well, that art has no purpose beyond the purely aesthetic, that it cannot thrive constrained by moral or social demands. "The artist is not responsible to anyone," claims Georg Baselitz, the German neo-expressionist painter. "His social role is asocial . . . . There is no communication with any public whatsoever. The artist can ask no question, and he makes no statement; he offers no information, message, or opinion. He gives no help to anyone, and his work cannot be used."

This is an attitude that began to take hold in America during the 1950's in the community of artists out of which Abstract Expressionism emerged. It was then that the totally self-possessed, self-reliant individual became the model for the typical artist in modern times. The gesture of putting paint on canvas became the ultimate gesture of liberation, not only from political and social norms, but from previous art history as well. History (which implies a responsibility to the past and a dependence on the achievements of others) was the obstacle to be transcended. A new art was necessary, and according to Barnett Newman, ". . . we actually began . . . from scratch, as if painting were not only dead but had never existed." At that point, modernism so embraced the notions of freedom and autonomy that we now have whole generations of artists who doubt that art was ever meant to be integrated with society's needs or purposes in the first place.

Certainly, much time has been spent during recent decades in denying that art has anything to do with either spiritual or ethical values. This is one of the things that makes contemporary modern art a thing for which there is, on the whole, no historical analogy—

this act of the will which consists in man's shutting himself off against any "higher" reality or divine life. But conspicuously missing in this "demystified" art is the sacramental vision that had been present in art for nearly all of human history; in the past, the world was enchanted. As material and rationalist values have gained pre-eminence, however, spiritual values have declined in direct proportion. The kind of sacramental vision to which I am referring is not that of routine church-going or religious dogma as such, but a mode of perception which incorporates the spiritual dimension. It is what Theodore Roszak has called "the Old Gnosis," a visionary style of knowledge, as distinct from a theological or factual one, that is able to see the divine in the human, the infinite in the finite, the spiritual in the material.

This very conception has largely been lost to artists in the late twentieth century. Freud may have rejected religion as neurotic illusion, judging the world of myth and magic negatively as errors to be refuted and supplanted by science, but such illusions have been positive and life-supporting, providing civilizations with their cohesion, vitality, and creative powers. And where they have been dispelled, there has been uncertainty and a loss of equilibrium— nothing to hold on to. If we accept as accurate Erich Fromm's description in *The Sane Society* of those human needs which are basic and essential—the need for relatedness, for transcendence (a concept which, for Fromm, has nothing to do with God, but refers to the need to transcend one's self-centered, narcissistic, alienated position in order to become related to others and open to the world), the need for rootedness, for a sense of identity, and for a frame of orientation and an object of devotion—then the achievements of modernism would appear to have been had at too high a cost. Too much that is crucial to human well-being will have been renounced, all in the name of freedom and self-sufficiency.

The practical consequences of this loss were described by the American painter Bruce Boice, in an address to students last year at the School of Visual Arts, entitled *What It Means to be an Artist*: "After leaving school," he said, "students often don't work because there's no reason to work. Nobody pays attention any more; so there seems no reason to press on. There's never a reason to do art work . . . it all looks all right, but it just doesn't matter. You get bored doing it because you're in a vacuum. There's no motivation; there are no rules to say what you should do, or whether it's good or not. Confidence is the thing that allows you to work eventually—you know you can do this thing and succeed at it. It gets harder all the time, but you get more used to the frustration. If there were rules, it would be simple enough to know what to do. But you find yourself looking for something, and you don't know what it is. So how do you ever know when you find it?"

I need hardly point out how this underlines the core weakness of the modernist ethos—the retreat into privatism and self-expression—which means that there is no example to follow, no authority to rely on, no discipline to be received. Individuality and freedom are undoubtedly the greatest achievements of modern culture. They have been crucial steps in the development of human consciousness: our emergence from instinctive or reactive consciousness and from the tribal mind. The problem, as I perceive it now, is that modernism has failed to understand individuality as something to be cultivated for the sake of something else. Insistence upon absolute freedom for each individual leads to a negative attitude toward society. If freedom is the absolute value, then society limits, and even frustrates, what is most essential and desirable. Freedom and social obligation are experienced in our culture as polar opposites which run at cross-purposes to each other. Beyond a certain point, freedom—like technological progress—becomes counterproductive: it defeats its own ends and becomes socially and spiritually alienating.

Until the modern epoch, all art had a social significance and a social obligation. To suggest that classical art was concrete but indentured and that modern art is free but abstract is merely to point out that impulses to autonomy and individualism run counter to processes of socialization and tradition. Abstract art brought into being not only a new aesthetic style, but also a change of understanding regarding the very raison d'etre of art itself. When art had a social role, when artists knew clearly what art was for, it didn't function in terms of self-interest. But with the breakdown of social consensus, it has become harder and harder to know what to choose or how to defend or validate one's choice. The freedom from all determinants leads to an indeterminacy so total that, finally, one has no reason for choosing anything at all. As Dane Rudhyar observed, the curious thing is that a culture simply breaks down when everything becomes possible—morally, metaphysically, scientifically, and socially.

As the sociologist Peter Berger has pointed out, "Modern consciousness entails a movement from fate to choice." Choice is a modern idea—there was no choice in traditional societies. To us, our relativistic philosophy may seem more appealing, but it seems to have a deeper biologic against it, in that too much freedom has distinctly negative consequences for the emotional economy of the individual. The "anguish of choice," which Fromm has written about so eloquently, can become a burden and a danger, since everything now depends on the individual's own effort. In taking away our faith in tradition, and our respect for authority, modernity has made us all fearful about belief in anything. It has made us isolated and anxious and has denied us the certainty of being part of some larger purpose. We take this absence of superior forces to be liberating, preferring autonomy, but the cost of such freedom has been the loss of security that comes from tradition and from a sense of communal purpose, which would normally guarantee for art both moral and practical significance. Indeed, according to Fromm, insecurity is what breeds the compensatory craving for fame and the compulsive striving for success.

The environmental anguish of the earth has entered our lives in such a way that the needs of the planet and the needs of the individual have become one. The issue arises with particular force in the context of current art-making, for if the experience and ideology of the unique and separate self, which has informed the stylistic practice of modernism, is over and done with, then it is no longer clear what artists and writers of the postmodern period are supposed to be doing. If the previous archetype of a "rugged" but alienated and suffering individual—the artist as heroic rebel and witness to contemporary despair—which has been the model in modern times, has become obsolete, then we need a new model, one that suggests a new principle of relatedness between artists and society. Such a model is one that breaks down thought patterns and energy forms which contribute to divisiveness, self-orientation, competition, and greed and reconnects us with the sacred stream.

All this said, I am not advocating a reversion to reprisals, paganism, or some other kind of religious revival. But our evolutionary agenda does suggest that we are all being tested, and that unless we undergo a change of consciousness and somehow acquire the moral will to reverse our present tendencies of seeing the world paranoically in terms of objects to be consumed and enemies to be annihilated, we will not survive as a species.

Modern Western society seems to be unique in regarding its art as a commodity to be sold in exchange for money, prestige, and power.

Aboriginal societies, for instance, did not perceive art in terms of its commercial value—no preindustrial culture ever did. Art was a living thing—a means of coming into contact with the life-force of nature—not something to be sold at a profit. In his book *The Gift*, Lewis Hyde claims that, in its fundamental nature, art is a gift and not a commodity. The idea of making art for profit only appears when spiritual, moral, and economic life begin to be separated from one another; it is this that marks the distinction between a gift-giving society and a market society. So it is hardly an accident that we call those nations known for their commodities the "free world." The phrase doesn't refer to political freedoms; it merely indicates that the dominant form of exchange in these lands does not bind the individual in any way—to family, to community, or to the state. It is only when a part of the self is *given* away that community appears. In the West, we are taught to sell ourselves, not to give ourselves away. A market atmosphere, with its constant demands for something new, is highly unfavorable to the creation of authentic and permanent values.

Today, there is still a pervasive sense that only by divorcing themselves from any social role can artists establish their own individual identity. But it strikes me that, as the dangers to planetary survival escalate, the practical consequences of such an attitude are becoming increasingly apparent. Our modernist notions of freedom and autonomy, of art answering only to its own laws, the pure aesthetic without a function, begin to seem a touch ingenuous. We simply cannot remain committed to our disembodied ideals of individualism, freedom, and self-expression while everything else in the world unravels. For those working in the area of cultural change, it has become necessary to explore the possibility that planetary survival and self-realization are only possible if we come to recognize the principle of interrelatedness—that everything exists in a unified field of being.

Although the shift into this more holistic framework is already visible in many other fields, in the case of artists, any impulse that challenges individuality or freedom tends to find itself up an emotional brick wall. To highly individualistic human beings, culturally conditioned to defend their right to freedom and self-expression above all else, the idea that creative activity might answer a collective cultural need, rather than a personal desire, is likely to appear irrelevant or even presumptuous. In my own thinking, art can no longer continue to be made in utter disregard of our planetary crisis.

This is not a call to social activism so much as a call to psychic awareness. The threat of extinction to our species by the prospect of both nuclear and ecological catastrophe suggests that perhaps the time has come to question our priorities, to awaken our hearts to the long-term effects of a rigid diet of aesthetic specialism. For the hidden constraint of an "art-for-art's sake" philosophy is that it has led the artist to cultural powerlessness.

So whether or not art has the power to change the world is no longer the appropriate question. The world is changing already; things are moving into a new mode because they have to; cultural awakening is being triggered by stress. As artists creating the future then, what is our responsibility and how can we fulfill it? Social renewal depends, ultimately, on individuals. But the powers necessary to save ourselves cannot be developed without an optimistic effort of will and an inward determination to meet the challenge of responsibility now posed to us all. Those who are prepared to make this effort are not the skeptics, the ones without faith, but those who share a vision of something worth saving. It is this consecrating of our individual selves to some greater enterprise, one that is aligned with a positive future and the well-being of the planet as a whole, that I take to be the crucial challenge to human creativity at this point. Like everyone else, artists can choose to undertake the transpersonal role, oriented to planetery purposes and the creative challenge of transformation; or they can remain culture-bound to the ego-ambitions of career, money, and success, and the pursuit of disembodied goals like "freedom" and "self-expression."

The precondition for any human effort is a vision of success. One way to make art into a culturally useful tool might be, then, to implant images of hope, images which can empower, into the collective unconscious. Symbols are evocative; they are transformers and conductors of psychic energies; they set into motion unconscious psychological processes; they have an integrating value and can evoke positive feelings. We will determine which future we create by the views and images we hold now. If art has a social function, it is, perhaps, to show humanity its optimal parameters.

First comes realization; then transformation. This, I have come to believe, is the true function of art: to become the instrument of transformation. Within each of us lies the potentiality for change. "Let there be transformation," says Marilyn Ferguson, "and let it begin with me." This is creativity in the deepest sense of the term.

And, as David Spangler points out, we are being asked not only to be experiencers and observers of change, but the actual architects of change. We are being asked to challenge the erroneous beliefs and assumptions which are now promoting annihilation. Now that we can see the mistakes and limitations of our past, we can make new patterns, new paradigms. Any artist who can see this and is capable of knowing that he or she is one of those magical figures who can command spirits, who can make contact with the source of meaning and power as our ancestors did, has already taken the first step toward transformation.

The need for innovation in art exists as much as ever, but its challenge at this point surely lies in more comprehensive goals that link the personal with the global. To effect such a paradigm-shift in our thinking will involve forging new purposes for art rather than new forms, that modernist obsession which has led, finally, to an empty worship of style. To claim a new relationship to art, to the world, and to ourselves is to realize that it is ourselves, rather than the world, that is in need of changing. To succeed at this, the form of our vision must be spiritual and compassionate; it must tap the mighty "something" of which we have been so tragically bereft—that living force which, if treated properly, and with respect, and if ceremonially fed, will give power to its owners.

James Hubbell

James Hubbell is an artist, sculptor, and designer-builder. With an intuitive, nature-sensitive approach, he has designed and built three restaurants, several homes, and a chapel. Over the years, his greatest volume of commissioned work has been in stained glass. The most exciting opportunity unfolded in 1982 when he was asked to create eighteen doors for a sheik's palace in Abú Dhabi. The jewel-like stained glass, metal, and woodwork was captured lyrically in the book, *The Doors of Abú Dhabi*, by Otto Rigan. (A portion of one of those windows was used for the cover of this book.) In 1980, the San Diego Board of Supervisors proclaimed a James Hubbell Day in recognition of his artistic contributions to San Diego County where he resides, calling him " . . . a diversified creative phenomenon, a contemporary Renaissance man living in our eclectic age." Mr. Hubbell and several friends started the Ilan-Lael Foundation in 1982 to promote aesthetic and holistic values in the development of the San Diego area.

*During a visit to San Diego several years ago, I was encouraged
by a mutual friend to see James' home, which is situated on a hill
and consists of small dwellings of the most inventive organic
shapes. Each one complements the natural environment and
each, in turn, is a world filled with the most wonderful creations,
from doors and windows to tiled floors and faucets, all crafted
with joyful imagination. This interview was held there in May of
1984.*

*   *   *

*What is the process you go through in creating an artwork—a
house, a sculpture, a stained-glass window, the swimming pool
by which we sit. How does it all start?*

The process begins with the part of me that is empty, the part I am
trying to fill. Without an inner kind of desire, the process has
nowhere to start. Art is learning how to be quiet; it's learning how to
listen to what a given situation wants to say; it's a conversation. I do
a drawing, I put a line down, and it says, "Put a curved line next to
me." I just feel that it wants me to do that. I don't come to art with a
plan; I don't come to the straight line telling it what to do.

*In your architectural work, for example, do you go to the site where
you will build and stay there for a while?*

Often when I'm working for somebody, and I'm going to do a
restaurant, for instance, they'll show me this absolutely ghastly old
building and say, "Look at this great thing!" I feel a sense of panic;
what can I do with this thing? As I get older and have had that
happen enough—the experience of the sheet of paper in front of me
with nothing on it, and the job that doesn't look solvable—I know
that there is a solution.

I first try to find out what the owner wants. He wants a restaurant;
he needs so many seats; he doesn't have much money . . . and I'm
going to have to do it by training the waiters to work on the building
or something like that. The problems that are in the building are
like the trees in a forest: if you can see them, if you look at them
without prejudice, they can tell you where the path is. After I find
out as much as I can, I get a feeling for what the building is going to
be: it's going to have horizontal lines, or there are deep shadows and

16

I want to use a curving line at the bottom and a soaring line at the top—all these things that give me the right feeling. I look for the language of this particular building.

How do you know that you've made the right decisions?

There are things that can't be done because of costs or technical requirements, and also, there are time limitations. If there are fifty right ways, there are a thousand wrong ways to do the building. So, what I try to do is to get close to what feels right. How do I know? I guess I get something in mind and say, "Boy, I'd like to see that." And that's enough.

We are at your home now. Because there were no pre-existing buildings here, was the process slightly different?

It was different in that the client was myself, and the time was mine; I could be extravagant with it if I wanted to. But it's not different in how I think about it. And sometimes limits can force better things.

This place is very beautiful. It reminds me of the old European villages. Obviously, what went into building this cluster of dwellings was guided by your sensitivity to nature and to function. Can you say anything more about these decisions?

There are many influences that affect every one of them. I think the thing that allows my newer buildings to be more free is the discipline that I have gained. As I know the materials and their limitations, I learn to do things with them which may not at first seem possible.

Do you feel that your creations get progressively better? Or are there some earlier things that stand out which you wish you could go back to—maybe the innocence, the purity, the directness of a form?

I don't think they get better. You used the words "innocence" and "purity." If you look at the art of little kids, you see they never do anything "wrong"; they haven't learned yet that they can make a mistake. So they put the line down because they believe in it. Part of

17

Various structures that make up the Hubbell home on the crest of the hill named Ilan-Lael. All photos of Hubbell's work by Otto B. Rigan.

The Waldorf School in Sacramento, CA, designed by Hubbell.

20

being an artist and spending years and years doing drawings is that you begin to believe that what you're doing needs to be done. It takes time to learn this. When you put a line down, you put it down because that's the way God wanted it to be. So, in a way, what you're learning is what kids are born with.

Do you feel in your own work that you are coming back to that childlike expression?

Yes . . . well, I don't know. You'd have to ask other people that question. My work is probably a lot more complex than it was, and it's also more refined. For example, if I am doing a restaurant, what I am looking for is the language of the restaurant. I look at the situation, at the possibilities and, in the process, a way emerges that can blend the given situation with what I imagine is possible. This way becomes the basic language for the structure. Once it is discovered, care must be taken not to skip into a different language—you can't use Spanish and Chinese together because no one will understand you. But when I've found the language, I've really answered almost everything there is in the building. I know something about the sinks and doors because the language that binds those into a unit is all there. That's what I try to do each time, and that's why I say I don't believe in style; I think style and language come out of the situation.

In our previous conversations you have used the analogy of leaves growing on a tree: they find their own best, unique way to grow.

The tree has its own language and cannot fail when it acts out of that language. So, once I get into the spirit of a place, whatever comes out of it is right and has integrity.

The way we tend to build today often dishonors and violates both the natural and the human community. Are you at all compelled in your work to balance that and correct it?

I think the artist acts like a raw nerve for the culture, suffering because of plagues, wars, and other things. But the artist has to live in the world, so his first solution is to try to make the world livable for himself. So he makes things—poems or pieces of music—which are for him a way to connect to the world, to say, "This is where I

21

belong, and I accept it." The artist can't go out and say, "I'm going to solve other people's problems." His work has to begin with himself because the problems are his. Later, other people might use the patterns of what he has found in solving their own problems.

When you look around at the works of other artists, do you see things that you feel are inspiring or done well, done in the way that those lines that you spoke of are right?

There are individuals whose work I like, but I don't find a lot of it very exciting. I really would like to be able to build a building that is like Mozart's music.

How is that?

I don't know. But what he did with music is so gorgeous and so real to me that somehow I'd like to do a building like that. But I don't yet know how to do it . . . .

I like to use materials and weave them back and forth. To me, tile isn't separate from cement, and cement isn't separate from glass; they all flow together. Very often architects are taught that there are parts of a building, and putting all the parts together makes a building. Economic considerations are usually at the top, function comes next, and aesthetics are down at the bottom. What we are discovering today is that they're all one thing; they all have to go together. In order for a building to be whole, it should have everything in it that people are made of. It should have all their dreams; it should have their history. I'm not saying that you list them that way, but that feeling should be there, should be included.

You mentioned in an earlier conversation that a lot of what you do is, in a sense, very individualistic. We talked about group work versus individual work, and you said that you would opt for individual work. You need certain space; you need to be account-able to your own self. Yet, you work with other people here. How do those two things come together?

I defend individuals because they are often taken superficially. The ideal thing is a balance between the community, or the group, and the individual. In a city of thousands, individuals are the important thing. If you begin thinking that the city is important and the individuals are not, then you have problems.

*In some ways your place here works like a medieval guild or
workshop: you are the master with several apprentices. Do you
ever think of yourself in that way?*

I like working with people. I work with craftspeople who are very
good and I like giving them a great deal of freedom in what they are
doing to express themselves.

*Do you make most of the decisions yourself, or do you trust others
enough to make them?*

At a certain point I have to trust, and it depends a lot on the
circumstance. Sometimes I have no other choice, and it may not
always work out; and sometimes it works out even better. In stained
glass work there's a certain grain to the glass and a certain direction
of the color, of value change in every sheet. In every piece of lead
there's a different size, a different way that the joining can be made.
There are hundreds of little decisions—I couldn't make each one. I
have to trust that others care about it and are willing to learn
enough to make it work together.

You honor their individuality in the process.

Absolutely. Part of it is realizing what they are capable of, not
giving them things that are impossible for them to do, but giving
them things that push them, so they can keep growing.

*If I would say to other people, "You have to see the work of James
Hubbell," where would you send them? Which work are you most
pleased with or best represents what you are about? Is it this
place?*

Yes, because this is where I've spent the most time—twenty-six
years. We're trying to figure out how to show that what we've done
here is a way of thinking about life; it's not the only way, but it is a
way that has relevance to other places.

I think it's a really exciting time for the world. For many people the
world is falling apart; the things they have believed in are no longer
appropriate. For an artist, a cathedral that is falling down has all
those bricks with which to build! The thing that is so exciting about
living now is that there are ways to rebuild our world. We have a

chance to watch the seeds, the first sprouts out of the ground, and
it's tremendously exciting.

*When you think ahead, do you have a sense of what there is for
you to do yet in this lifetime, of what is being called out from you
that may be different from what you have done so far?*

I don't know specifically. The first period of my life was very
introverted. I barely talked to anybody for the first twenty-five years.
Then I went through twenty-five years of having jobs, having a
family, and learning about the rest of the world. For the last five
years or so, I seem to be working in a bigger world. A lot of my work
is outside of San Diego, in different countries. I would like to take a
show to Russia, for example.

*Do you feel that there is more growth for you, that there is more for
you to learn?*

Absolutely. At certain points I am terrified that there might not be
any more gifts. I don't know if this is the last thing I'll do or if there
will be anything else. So I have to live each day and hope that it will
keep happening.

Are "gifts" available to only certain people?

No, I think they're for anybody. I'll put it this way: if I had the
choice of seeing a kid that was really talented, who had all the gifts
that could make a great artist, and somebody that just worked like a
dog, I'd put my money on the person that worked like a dog. I worked
for a school for crippled children, and there was a little Black boy
who didn't have any legs and only one hand and a hook. And he
would ride a tricycle; he'd sit on the bumper and run the pedal with
the hook and steer with the hand. And he would fall off the bike, and
bounce around, and laugh, and just have the greatest time. Other
kids, who had smaller problems, would just sit and look at the wall.
He taught me that it's not what you have; it's what you do with what
you have.

What is the motivation behind taking a show to Russia?

Like everybody else, I worry about the relationship between the US
and Russia and I think, in a sense, it's unreal. It's like we're working

through some mythology that we don't understand. I read a book called "The Land of the Firebird," a cultural history of Russia. It gave me such a different picture of who the Russian people are than what I had always been led to believe. That was the big thing. In nature, if you take a rock and put it on the grass and then, days later, take it off the grass, the grass will have turned yellow. But the grass will often grow taller in that spot. I think that is possible in a place like Russia. If the right things happen, if the right people and right kind of openings are there, Russia might have a tremendous amount to give to the world.

Somehow the dream has to be resurrected that there's a light at the end of the tunnel, and where we are going is tremendously exciting. All that the artist can do is to say that there is a light in this world, that there is a way out, and that it's really exciting. Sometimes what we think are the hardest things to do are actually the easiest; everybody has avoided them, thinking that they are not possible. But the door may really be all the way open.

For further information about James Hubbell's work, contact the Ilan-Lael Foundation, P.O.Box 4871, San Diego, CA 92104.

Matthew Fox is an author, lecturer, and theologian, prominently featured at universities and religious and cultural conferences throughout the United States and Canada. He has published approximately sixty articles on spirituality in theological, cultural, and religious journals in North American, English, French, and Dutch journals. He has authored ten books, amongst them *Western Spirituality: Historical Roots, Ecumenical Routes*; *Breakthrough: Meister Eckhart's Creation Spirituality in New Translation*; and *Original Blessing: A Primer in Creation-Centered Spirituality*. Matthew holds Masters degrees in both Philosophy and Theology and a Doctorate in Spirituality, received Summa Cum Laude, from the Institut Catholique de Paris. Presently he is Director of the Institute in Culture and Creation-centered Spirituality at Holy Names College in Oakland, California.

*I had heard of Matthew Fox and the value of his work for several
years before I actually heard him speak at Saint John the Divine
Cathedral in New York. He spoke of a theology that places creativity at its very center, and I was struck by the great passion and
clarity that he gave to the subject. In May, 1984, I stopped by his
office in Oakland for the following interview.*

*   *   *

*I would like to begin with questions about creation-centered
theology. How does it differ from other theologies, and how is it
relevant to the issue of creativity and the arts?*

In the Creation tradition, creativity is understood to be the
reflection of God in people—the capacity to birth images and the
ability to choose certain ones to express. All of Creation is seen as
creative from the moment of the "Great Light" (taken from Brian
Swimme, instead of the "Big Bang," which is so macho a name for
the origin of creation.) The entire universe has been creating
constantly. Every morning there's more creation. As Meister
Eckhart, the key spokesperson in the Creation tradition, puts it,
"Only the human soul is generative like God is." So, although all life
is generative and creative, the factors that are unique to the human
condition are the capacity to choose and reject images and the
incredible fertility of imagination.

Creativity is precisely the ground where humanity and divinity
share common space, the very core of human and divine union. The
Creation tradition, therefore, puts art (with a small "a") in the center
of the development of the human person and of the satisfaction of
human culture. As Eckhart would put it, there is no work that is
satisfying to the human being that is not essentially a work of
creativity, and each of us has this potential for self-expression—
living out images—which is what art is all about.

So, a very essential part of the Creation tradition is to critique art,
because just as the human imagination can be God-like, it can also
border on the demonic. We can use our creativity to make more and
more Trident submarines and laser weapons, or we can use it to put
people to work, to celebrate life, to create music, and folk art, and
rituals that heal the human condition and its relationship to the
rest of creation. When you really get down to the importance of
creativity, you're getting down to priorities and choices and whether

those choices are for life or for death. All of this has really been quite explicit in the Creation tradition.

In the other Western tradition—the Fall/Redemption tradition, which is far better known, unfortunately—creativity plays no role at all. You can read voluminous books on spirituality in which the word creativity is not mentioned once. In that tradition, control and perfection are major categories, not birthing and creativity.

I think that for a theology to celebrate creativity, it must have a sense of the Motherhood of God. An exclusively paternalistic theology—which is what the West has had for three centuries, speaking and imaging God only as male—doesn't celebrate birthing, doesn't see birthing as the powerful, exciting, surprising, ecstatic, and spiritual event that it is, personally and culturally. In the Creation tradition, people like Mechtilde of Magdeburg, Meister Eckhart, Julian of Norwich (one of the founders of the English language), and Hildegard of Bingen all image God explicity as Mother, not just as Father. This is very important, and I think there will be no awakening of the artist in people until there is a letting go of the exclusively patriarchal images of Divinity. As true art is awakened, there will be a return to the more ancient traditions that celebrate God as Mother at least as much as Father.

The put-down of the artist has corresponded with the put-down of the feminine side of God. And again, theologically, the Creation tradition is the oldest tradition in the Hebrew Bible, as well as in the New Testament. What life did Jesus choose, after all? He was an artist, a story-teller; he created parables. He even created the form of the parable, which was a take-off of the midrash. He has been called everything else in Christianity—King, Priest, Teacher, Saviour— but essentially his life-style was that of an artist. And this has been missed by so many Christians that it demonstrates how the very meaning of art has been repressed in Western civilization and in Western religion.

You quoted Eckhart's statement about the dignity and satisfaction of human beings coming out when it is born from within, when it is creative. By that standard most people in our culture are not exercising and celebrating their Divinity, but are only externalizing other people's thoughts or ideas. It appears that few people are really masters of their own lives in that way.

That's very true, and it is one of the tragedies of our time. All of advertising, I think, is built on taking in someone else's images,

29

which are often high-powered, expensive, and put together by people with great artistic talent. Television, of all the media, has this great potential for beauty or ugliness, liberation or slavery. I think that a lot of people are being enslaved by the media today. They're not being encouraged by the media or by our other institutions—government, education, politics, and religion—to create or birth the images inside themselves and to take responsibility for them.

Doesn't it take an incredible amount of courage to begin with listening instead of taking in ready-made images?

It's what the mystics would call the "via negativa." Again, the Fall/Redemption tradition reduced the "via negativa" to asceticism, beating oneself up, which is not what it means. In the Creation tradition the "via negativa" is the letting go of images, becoming empty, in order that newness and fullness might be birthed. That kind of meditation is found in Zen Buddhism, for example, and also in Eckhart and the Creation tradition of the West.

It's a dialectic, though. On the one hand, the artist must be in love with life, must be delighted, and turned on, and excited. I think that's the artist's role: to excite the community about love of life and an awareness of what is endangering life. But there's another side which involves letting go of one's most cherished images of life in order to be with the silence, the darkness, the imagelessness—true emptiness. Out of that emptiness, creativity comes. So I see it as a dialectical process of embracing images and letting go of images.

If emptying is the first stage of the artistic process, what would be the second?

Emptying is the second stage. I think the first stage is falling in love—falling in love with life and what I call the "via positiva." There are exceptions. But I think that's the combination for creativity—the "via positiva" plus the "via negativa"—falling in love with life and then the willingness to let go. Meister Eckhart creates a beautiful image of that when he says, "I had a dream that I was pregnant, even though a man pregnant with nothingness. And out of this nothingness, God was born." The whole sense of embracing the dark and the nothingness is the source of fruitfulness.

So there is the falling in love with life and then the emptying. But art has to do with creating forms. What follows?

Well, until one is emptied of forms, forms cannot be created, only borrowed from other people. That's not art; that's reformation. So the artist must really be involved with renewal. Out of the first two elements—falling in love with life, or cherishing life, and then emptying—comes the imaging. There are many ways in which this happens. One is through the recycling of materials, using materials in ways that have never been thought of before. I think many artists do that: poets do it with words, musicians do it with chords.

It's useful to be able to name these stages because it allows us to clear away the junk that the human race has dumped on children and adults to prevent creativity. The fact is that it is very natural to be creative. Look at children: they can make up a game in a snap, provided they haven't spent all their lives in front of a television set taking in other peoples' images instead of exercising their own imaginations. The capacity to image is natural. There is much in our culture that has taught us to repress imaging: religion itself tells us that some images are good, others are bad, some are acceptable and some are unacceptable. Such mores prevent creativity.

What about artists who go through those inner stages but produce what is not necessarily good art? Don't you think that the practice of the artist must also include a kind of crafting, an attentiveness to how forms are created and put together?

Yes! The making of the form itself is a tremendously creative act, and the form has to be created and re-created every time for the true artist. I know, for myself as a writer, that the best part of my books is always the table of contents because it is my form, my structure. I have to dream many, many nights before the table of contents comes to me. I can have all kinds of matter, and material, and content, but I know that until the table of contents comes to me and I have the correct structure, I do not have a book. It is the form that is so essential.

Jesus was brilliant as an artist in that he could create new teachings with familiar images. He was able to communicate in a manner that was very appropriate to the people with whom he spoke. Appropriateness seems to be very important in any form of communication.

Yes. I think all authentic art that is serving community must essentially be folk art, that is, art for the folks and not for investors or the elite. In looking at Western art, what we have called the "great works" have more often than not been done in a very non-elitist way or out of a non-elitist quest. I suspect that most artists, if given a chance, would like their work to affect the ordinary people in a culture, to enlighten and enliven their love of life and their cherishing of it. But the recent history of artists has been one of bare survival and of having to compromise or associate with some kind of patron—a corporation buying advertising, for example. It's a pity that some of our best artists go that way, getting us to buy more things instead of to cherish what already is.

So, folk art is centrally an issue of spirituality: eliciting the artist in every person and allowing every person to cherish the beauty that others in the human race have birthed. What we're trying to do here in our Institute is to get ordinary people—and by ordinary I mean those people who have no great talent in one form of art or another—to realize that they can center their lives around birthing, be it dance or play or painting or massage.

What do you do here in order to evoke people's creativity?

The first thing we do is remove what has been taught from kindergarten: that there is "good" and "bad," that there are grades—A,B,C,D, or F—and that there is a "right" or "wrong" way to do something. We have to move people out of that mind-set of judgment into a mystical mind-set in which everything is gratuitous anyway; they're already loved and they don't have to earn their living or their justification by how well they do the art. It's a whole different approach. Once this is done, amazing things will happen, especially with adults. The key, as Eckhart says, is to develop "unselfconsciousness," which Jesus has said is to "become like a child." If you can't help adults to become like children again, they will not create art that is truly satisfying; they'll do it to please someone outside. Once you relieve the burden of guilt, the judgment, and the comparisons to someone else's art, amazing things begin to flow.

But for most people, what is created is relevant only to their own lives. It seems that those whose art is relevant outside themselves are rare. There is a personal folk art—getting in touch with creativity—but there are other levels of art in which the artist is a voice for a community or a culture. The two are not necessarily the same. Do you agree?

A second dimension of entering art as meditation is letting go of the notion of art as product and returning to the non-capitalist notion that art is basically process. The process itself is the "way." The "way" is the "way." And then you can say, "Oh my! There is a product." But that is really secondary. It is the process of the artist becoming an artist, getting in touch with his or her powers of creativity, that is the important thing. When you're talking about art that would imbue the community, you're not just talking about art objects; you're talking about the artist. The best thing the artist creates is the artist.

If you are awakening ordinary people to their own creativity, they are going to become better citizens, better parents, better educators, more imaginative solvers of human problems and conditions. They might not be able to create a sculpture that is going to stand in the middle of town, but they may become politicians or lawyers who recreate social structures, or parents who raise gifted or un-gifted children. You can't control art; if it is truly art, it is full of surprises. And the surprise of getting adults in touch with their own creativity is that we don't know what it will mean, because it has been such a rare phenomenon in Western culture of late.

As you open people up to trust their own images and creativity, they will come to respect the gifts of "special" artists more deeply. In other words, following a true folk art awakening will be more work for full-time artists. But such artists must themselves let go of professionalism and enter their work as conscious enablers of society's dreams and visions. There is no such thing as a "personal" art expression, if by personal you mean cut-off from community. The deeper, more truthful the expression of one's own journey, one's own depth of pain and joy, the more immediately it is recognized by others who are in touch with their own pain and joy. It's the process again, and I think it is a very narrow and dual- istic understanding of art that would suggest that there is a public and a private contribution made by art. I am not denying that there are degrees of gifts, but if ordinary people are in touch with their artistry, the work world, and neighborhoods, and homes that we live in will be recreated. I think that is a very essential part of folk art.

So far we have talked about the creative process and the creative potential within each human being. At the same time there are, for lack of a better term, "cultural" artists, people who seem to attune so deeply to the rhythm of their world that they become a voice for a larger group of people. Can you give examples of such artists?

I think of Rilke, whose poetry is a prophetic expression of human spirituality in wonderful images. I think Adrienne Rich's poetry is very powerful and prophetic, awakening us to that lost wisdom of women's experience in particular. I see someone like Gandhi as a great artist, an artist at organizing people, Third-World colonized people, to assert their dignity and rights. And then, of course, there is his disciple, Martin Luther King, who did the same thing in this country. Gustav Mahler, in the field of music, said so much about the depths of twentieth century pathos and yearning. Many musicians—Wagner, Schumann, Mozart, Bach, and Stravinsky, to name a few—have had so much spirituality, and love of life, and passion to share with us.

But we don't know how to listen to the great prophets in our life. That's why we are teaching people to realize that these great artists are speaking about the spiritual journey of us all. It's a very powerful thing. If we let go of the spectator approach to art, the capitalist approach to art, we realize that so many artists are gifts of the cosmos, waking us up to the truth of our lives. I've mentioned a few poets and musicians and political artists who mean a lot to me. They are all prophets. I suppose in previous generations they would have been called saints. They embody the archetypal needs of our times, the deep needs, the unspoken needs; they speak the ineffable.

In my concept for this book, I used the image of a cultural DNA, suggesting that each era has a gift to offer in the evolution of human history, and that artists stand forth and announce these gifts. Is that an acceptable image for you? If it is, what are some of the elements and qualities of our present DNA? What are the seeds out of which the future will grow?

Well, there is a global consciousness, the development of which is essential. We now realize that we are one village. The astronauts look back when they are up there and realize that there's no borderline between Russia, and Europe, and Canada, and the US; the rivers aren't marked "Communist," "Socialist," or "Capitalist." Nor are the oceans, the clouds, the air, or the earth. Nothing important is labeled with the labels that humanity has put on everything. So, there is a whole lot of letting go that has to happen. It's a new consciousness that is part of people all over the world; it is not restrictive based on social or economic class.

Science, too, is developing a new world story. To my understanding, every tribe has identified itself by its creation story. We now have a tribal creation story, based on science, that includes us all whether we be Russian, Indian, Chinese, European, American, or African. We're beginning to create one story, which has to do with twenty billion years of history. It is an amazing story about the birth of our species on this planet.

Ecumenism in the religions of the world is just in its baby-steps, but it is terribly important because there will be no global community without global spirituality. That the Catholic Church in the sixties could say, in its declaration on non-Christian religions, that the Holy Spirit works, and has always worked, through other religions and other cultures, is a major turnabout. Only a hundred years ago they were talking about no salvation outside of the Catholic Church!

But for ecumenism to really work, it has to reach the mystical level of religion. Religion is not only morality and doctrine, it is also mysticism. This is the level on which ecumenism has developed most slowly, probably because there has been so little mysticism in Western religion over the past three-hundred years. Again, I think our work here at ICCS is so important because we are uncovering the mystics that preceded the rationalistic period of Western culture: Eckhart, Hildegard, Julian, for example. Every place I go, mystics are coming out of the closet—lawyers, engineers, doctors, artists, poets, businessmen, and women. Even a few ministers and priests are awakening to the mystic in themselves. Young people, even teenagers, are demanding it. I think the interest in drugs and drink is a statement about how little mysticism exists in young people's lives.

And then, the coming together of science and mysticism is an ultimate necessity, because myths are born out of a cosmological world-view that is religious, and mysterious, and scientific. This is happening in our time with the letting go of Newton in science and of Augustine and the Fall/Redemption patriarchy in religion.

I think the quest for community is also part of the new DNA. The respect for diversity, the notion that there are many life-styles that are appropriate for the human species—married and monastic, single and celibate, with children and without children, heterosexual and homosexual. Prejudice against certain lifestyles has always been evident in Western history. Consider the prejudice

Protestants had against celibates for three-hundred years until the ecumenical movement, or the teachings of the churches against homosexuals. We should recognize that it is new, for our culture at least, to be celebrating diversity of lifestyles.

I associate all this with creativity and art. One of the important folk arts is the birthing of our styles of life and being responsible for them, being true to them and not judging them by outside standards. To reflect diversity is essential for all creativity. I welcome the work that is being done in developing community today. It is cutting across religious lines and heritages; it is obviously an essential need of the human species. I sense very strongly the desire to create universal rituals, to celebrate all of this in ritual. It is one of the really deep artistic needs of our times. This is folk art. It's listening and being attuned to the needs of people and their images. It heals the community deeply.

There is another element in all of this: in the emergence of a global culture, there is the possibility that all of the unique, aboriginal cultures will be destroyed in the process.

I think much of the wisdom we need will come, if we allow it, from the native peoples. They are in touch with a period of human consciousness which includes intuition, a more "matrifocal" approach to living, and ritual that has great power. The very genocide that has been done on these cultures demonstrates that the human race was projecting a fear of something repressed.

Otto Rank has done absolutely brilliant work on art and artists in our century, and he says that the number one obstacle to art is the fear of death. He says that Jesus and Paul brought about the biggest revolution that the world has ever seen: the Resurrection, the overcoming of the fear of death and, therefore, the liberation of creativity from within the human psyche. I find this to be an amazing thesis. And it is not partisan; it is coming not from a Christian, but from a Jew. He is saying that the fear of death, the fear of letting go, of mortality, is what prevents people from birthing and being creative. I think that the whole meaning of Resurrection has got to be explored by artists, not by theologians who have managed to reduce it to something boring and literal. I think it is going to take artists to really understand what Rank is about.

It is a unique theological contribution that the anawim, the poor, the little ones, contain much more art, and much more beauty and

Divinity than they are being given credit for. The liberation of the poor has everything to do with the liberation of the artist. Paulo Friere from Brazil writes that the poor struggle ". . . not only for the freedom from hunger, but also for the freedom to create." Again, that notion of moving art from the elite to everybody is essential to the survival of the global village, because it is essential for peaceful, and gentle, and satisfying living.

For further information about Matthew Fox's work, write: ICCS, Holy Names College, 3500 Mountain Blvd., Oakland, CA 94619.

Naj Wikoff

Naj Wikoff's active involvement of community in the creative process has earned him a national reputation as a sculptor and painter, artist-in-residence, and arts management consultant.He holds a B.F.A. from the Pratt Institute and an M.A. in Sculpture from Hunter College, and is represented in the collections of major corporations, including the Kemper Group and First Bank Systems, and the Zolla/Lieberman Gallery of Chicago. As Executive Director of the Dutchess County Arts Council in upstate New York, he founded that community's united arts fund and served as Vice-Chairman of the National Fine Arts Committee for the 1980 Winter Olympics in Lake Placid. He has also served as a development consultant to community arts agencies across the country.

I met Naj in 1981 in Madison, Wisconsin, where we had both been invited to address a conference of arts administrators at the University of Wisconsin School of Business. We met several times over the next year and discovered an affinity that brought us into working together to initiate the ETA Project. In 1982 I saw Naj's Prairie Ship and was fascinated by the monumental size of his sculpture, its beautiful integration with the rolling Wisconsin hills, and the process of involving the local community of Mount Horeb in the creative processes. This interview was held in September of 1985 when Naj visited me briefly in my home in Issaquah.

*   *   *

You are a sculptor. Can you describe your work and the method that you have adopted for that work?

The work that I do is not all that unusual or special. It's an exploration of light and form within an environment. The works are assembled, usually out of branches, out of fiber, out of found materials—materials that relate to the specific environment. I have been influenced by the early-American folk art techniques, particularly those that are anchored in the Adirondacks, like the rustic twig furniture. Perhaps what is most different about my work is that I often involve other people in the creative process. I take inspiration from folk tales and the language of a specific environment or culture. The whole gestalt of society interests me, and I try to involve all those elements in the creative process. This, perhaps, is different.

Could you give an example of a project that exemplifies this difference?

I was commissioned, in 1981, to create an environmental fabric sculpture in the Commons in Columbus, Indiana. Many of the buildings in Columbus, by the way, have been designed by world-class architects—sort of a "who's who" of architecture. Much of it doesn't really serve the community's needs though—or at least that was the impression that I got from many people there. So, before I designed anything, I talked to people in the community to learn about their history, and I found that they had a strong farming ethic. For example, almost every block in town had a 4H-type club where women would get together to quilt, can food, and do all sorts of co-operative activities that came out of their farming history. In designing the artwork, I involved these women as volunteers and created a three-dimensional quilt that both tied in with their roots and played off the geometric patterns of the architectural setting. It made the artwork very personal to them. And there were far more volunteers helping to fabricate the artwork than I could handle!

What kind of work did the volunteers do?

They did the cutting and sewing of fabric and helped make the wooden frames. They also shared their knowledge with me and improved my skills. So it was really a process of sharing skills, aesthetics, and social concerns.

Does the design for a work come from you, or do you involve other people in the design process?

The design of the work comes through me; my responsibility is to maintain the aesthetic standard. However, more and more I am trying to involve people in the design process. As I get older, I am more at ease with influences that alter my thinking and awareness; there are people who can "lobby" my aesthetics. At the same time, it is part of my work to help those people release their creativity and see the world differently. An example is a work in progress in Ogden, Utah, where I involved a cross-section of citizens who worked with me to collectively choose the criteria by which the site for the work, the materials, and so forth, were selected. At the same time, I was creating a context out of which their insights could be put into form. After designing the prototype, I took it back to the group, which again had its input, and so on.

Obviously, there is a lot of work connected with this approach that stretches out a process which otherwise could be much shorter. What are the benefits of this?

Part of my attitude toward the arts has been shaped by the fact that for three years I was the director of a community arts council in upstate New York. Prior to that time I worked in the traditional mode of an artist, doing my thing, and painting apartments, and driving taxis to support myself. And I hustled to put my art out there

41

in the galleries, museums, magazines. Directing the arts council helped me see artists and their work through the eyes of those who were impacted by the art—the community—and altered my artistic vision. Now I try to be more responsible to that environment. A gallery is a very pure space in which exploration can take place, but in creating artworks for public spaces, all sorts of new factors come into play. Now I ask myself, "What are the uses for the space? What happens around the space? Who are the people in the community, and what are their needs?"

What happened to the quilt in Columbus? Did it achieve what you hoped it would?

It was commissioned as a temporary work—the materials used were fabric and wood, not steel and marble. But it is still there; the community really came to like it. I feel that it was very successful.

Do you think people have the same connection with a work if they are not involved in the creative process?

With some works of art the connection is there; it depends on the sensitivity of the artist. I think that the artist can open the creative process for others, so people have a higher level of understanding of how to create things and take risks in their own lives. Also, through this process people get to know their community better, and each other, and concepts related to art and aesthetics.

Have you pretty much developed the language of your work by now? Are you going to continue in this vein?

Yes, very much so. What I give up is time by myself in the studio; involvement with volunteers and the amount of administration that these large installations require eats tremendously into the time available for my own creative work. On the other hand, it also provides an opportunity for a great deal more thinking about my work. Instead of doing four or five variations on a given theme, I end up choosing one. But that one is thought through much more thoroughly. Instead of happening in a few weeks, it takes a year or so. I'm not sad about the price I pay—the loss of private time— because I'm enriched by the people and have a greater responsibility to the environment and the materials I use and an increased awareness of the power and importance of the arts.

Can you say more about how you see the power of the arts?

One of the things I learned while running the Arts Council is that people want to get involved. Just to sit and watch an event or listen to a concert is somehow not enough. There is a need for people to touch each other and get involved. We have a lot of polarization in our society, a lot of shifts of power, and I think there is a greater need now for people to come together. The arts provide a fabulous way of doing this. By involving people in creative processes, I feel that I am responding to a need that exists in our society.

What are things you have learned about this process over the years?

Ten years ago I felt that I had to do every single thing in an artwork. I am learning to become more like a director in a movie, so that opening up the process is no longer a threat to my ego or my sense of ownership.

How did you accomplish that? Where did your ego go?

It has to do with confidence; I'm not insecure about many issues. My father's death also had quite an impact on me. It made me more generous. I used to have tunnel vision, particularly before I ran the Arts Council; I wanted to be a hot young artist who would make it in Soho and the Museum of Modern Art, and so forth. I was hustling galleries, and critics, and magazines in New York. Slowly my priorities started to shift and, after moving around the country some, I realized that New York is an important place for the arts, but not necessarily the end all and be all. I found out that there was enormous opportunity for artists in other parts of the country. So I started to explore those opportunities.

Often people see your work like Christo's. How do you respond to that?

I have a lot of respect for Christo's aesthetics, so I am flattered that people compare me with him. But our approaches are different. Simply put, you could say that his process is very clean, and mine is very messy. Generally, he selects his desired site, designs the proposed artwork, raises his own funds, and hires all the people who organize, fabricate, and install the artwork. It's a very straight-forward process. Naturally, working on this scale, he often has to launch quite a lobbying effort to gain the support or permission of the powers that be. But his vision is fairly absolute, and his work is either installed or not.

My approach is not that controlled. I usually respond to an invitation from a community and arrive with no preconceived notion of what I am going to do. I begin by meeting with as wide a cross-section of the community as possible, which leads to the formation of ad hoc committees or loose associations of people who wish to work with me. I get these groups involved in researching the unique character, culture, and climate of their region, which helps me develop criteria for the artwork and parameters for the site. Ultimately, these people generate the many volunteers who assist in the labor of putting the artwork together. We solicit in-kind dona-tions of materials and supplies and grants from foundations, corporations, community arts agencies, and individuals. Through my projects, I try to increase opportunities for local artists by pointing up the importance of the arts in the community rather than polarizing the community through controversy. I get very little criticism or antagonism from the press; there is no controversy. This process has by no means been perfected, but perhaps it is this difference in approach that sets my work apart from Christo's the most.

What is your current project?

It is called *Prairie Ship Liberty*, an environmental sail-sculpture based on the design of a frigate ship. It will be made of utility poles—tall pine poles stripped of branches for masts—and colorful nylon fabric for sails. In terms of design, the sails will play off the natural, cultural, and historical imagery of an area. In the North-west, for example, I will pay attention to the importance and impact of the volcanoes, the rich variety in climate that produces rainforest and desert, all within a two-hour drive, the powerful impact of the Native Americans of the Pacific Coast, and the Oriental residents. The *Liberty* will "sail and tack" across the country through a series of installations, beginning in Portland, Oregon, and ending in New York City where it will be an official entry in the Parade of Tall Ships as part of the Centennial Celebration of the Statue of Liberty. In each location the design of the sails will change slightly—in some

Prototype of Prairie Ship Liberty afloat in Mt. Horeb, WI, September, 1982.

Rendering of possible sail design: Northwest Coast - Chinese, Japanese, Northwest Indian.

45

areas more than others—with volunteers working on new sails which (to give you a sense of scale) are larger than a basketball court. By the time the *Liberty* reaches New York, the sails will form a giant mosaic representing the energy and vitality of the peoples that make up our nation. After New York, we plan to take the ship to France and give it to the French people, honoring them for their gift of the Statue of Liberty one-hundred years earlier.

Where is this project at this point in time?

The project really started in the spring of 1985 and came together very quickly. We now have eleven potential sites in this country and five in Europe. We're in the middle of a fundraising effort to create a financial base for all this to happen. By November we will be ready to focus on the specific designs and begin work with the communities.

Can you say more about your voyage to France?

I heard the Paul Winter Consort at the Cathedral of Saint John the Divine in December of 1984, and Paul was talking about "sky bridges" between various countries, especially between the Soviet Union and the United States. I asked myself what I could do, as an artist, to help build bridges. In mid-January I was approached by the organizer of the Parade of Tall Ships, who wanted to know whether I would be willing to bring my prototype prairie ship, created in Wisconsin in 1982, to New York in 1986. I thought about it and came back with a proposal to create a similar artwork that would "sail" to New York. And then, why end there? The Statue of Liberty came across the ocean from France; in fact, the French helped Americans raise money for the base of the sculpture. So it seemed to me that there needed to be a return gesture, and the idea came for us to take the *Prairie Ship Liberty* there and give it to the French in October, 1986, on the anniversary of the unveiling of the Statue of Liberty.

Do the French know about your plans?

Yes, I approached the French Embassy in May, and they were very pleased by the whole notion. They were, in fact, overwhelmed about it all. Since then they have been very helpful to us in seeking a site and host agency to welcome the ship to France.

Do you ever think, in the midst of all the work, about what comes after the Prairie Ship Liberty?

Oh yes. I want to create an artwork within the context of the Pacific basin. That means spending some time in China, in Japan, in Alaska, in western South America. On the one hand I think, "No, not another large-scale artwork!" But, on the other hand, I've always had a hankering to travel east. . . .

Introduction of Quilt and Star Pattern; Installation at New York Harbor.

For further information about Naj Wikoff's work, contact the ETA Project, P.O.Box 663, Issaquah, WA 98027.

William Irwin Thompson

William Irwin Thompson is a cultural historian, poet, novelist, and the Founding Director of the Lindisfarne Association, a non-profit educational organization dealing with issues of cultural history and planetary transformation. He has taught at the Massachusetts Institute of Technology, York University in Toronto, Canada, and the University of Hawaii. William has written extensively on issues of cultural transformation, including such books as *At the Edge of History, Evil and World Order, Darkness and Scattered Light, The Time Falling Bodies Take to Light, Pacific Shift*, and a novel entitled *Islands Out of Time: A Memoir of the Last Days of Atlantis*. Thompson currently lives and writes in Bern, Switzerland, and continues to travel to the United States for lectures and teaching assignments.

49

Over the years that I've known William, I've come to think of the way his mind works as like a Jackson Pollock painting: with dazzling speed he sweeps through history, dipping into the wells of myth and art, and splashing them onto the canvas of our current reality. His work is an illumination of evolutionary patterns, warning of the dangers and inspiring the possible. This interview was held in March of 1984 during a visit William made to the Lorian Association.

*   *   *

If we accept the assumption that within this time there is a new dispensation, a new spirit or DNA, how would you describe it? How do we recognize it?

I see it in terms of three historical phases. The first phase is the phase of the Great Mother, where humanity is surrounded, dominated, and overwhelmed by Nature, and consciousness is not really separate or individuated. The archetype of this phase might be the engraving of the *Venus of Laussel* from about fifteen-thousand B.C. This is the Great Mother with the enormous stomach and pendulous breasts holding up the bison horn, which is also the crescent moon. The child is still inside. She's covered over with red ochre, which is generally considered to be a symbol of the menstrual blood and the life-giving power of the woman.

The next phase is the emergence of an individuated psyche and consciousness, but one which sees the breaking away process as threatening its connection to the Mother, as frightening, terrifying, and sacrificial. The archetypal work of art that I see expressing this state of consciousness would be Michelangelo's *Pietá*. Here the son of the Great Mother is dead in her arms; consciousness is seen to be alienated from nature, dying tragically, crucified. The resolution between individuation and affiliation (in the literal Latin sense of the word "son") is not resolved harmoniously. But the Mother is now seen as closer in age and closer in body type or body style to the son.

The third phase I see as the erotic stage. Consciousness becomes a lover and the feminine is seen as the erotic consort, rather than the dominating mother. As equals, the male and female meet in a kind of ecstatic union so that consciousness now returns to understand Gaia and nature and ecology; male does not dominate female.

I suppose one could say that there was as sub-phase, the Christian, which could be called patriarchial, where the male attempts to kill the Great Mother and dominate the female. This is industrial society. In this phase we seem to want to get rid of the body through genetic engineering, to control reproduction scientifically in the laboratory. We want to get rid of the Earth and create an artificial environment in a space colony, make the planet a "spaceship Earth," as Bucky Fuller used to call it. I see that as the last gasp of a pathological orientation. But the future should be much more that of the orphic singer, the ecstatic return to the underworld to find the lover, the subterranean feminine, to bring it into some much more cyclical harmony.

So I see that art since the Renaissance has been serving the process of individuation. In classical, neo-classical, and early medieval times you didn't have autobiography; you didn't have novels about a person's thoughts. Chaucer didn't take himself as seriously as a modern artist would; Shakespeare didn't either. It's only after the Renaissance that you get attention to the individual as a value in and of himself, separate from the value given to him either by nature, or by the community, or by the church. Now, of course, we take this for granted. Since Romanticism, the voyage of consciousness, the poet on top of the mountain—like William Wordsworth communing with the stars on Mount Snowdon—is part of our heritage.

I think that the challenge now is to return the fully individuated consciousness to its matrix, whether we want to call that the universe, or the Great Mother, the planet Gaia, or whatever, and form an ecology of consciousness. Consciousness can find harmony with other consciousness, other beings, in some form of association. At the same time, it becomes part of the consciousness of the Earth as a living being or the Earth as a whole, without a sacrifice of individuation.

Most people still can't take the agony of individual consciousness. They feel the threat of death, of being cut off from the Great Mother, or they feel the threat of loneliness. So they look for the suppression of identity in a cult, wearing a uniform, or joining some form of totalitarian group. And that's pathological; that doesn't go anywhere. That's a reversal of the process. That's as futile as taking a ten-month-old child and trying to shove it back into the womb. It's not healthy, even for the mother. If we are the sensing mechanism, the brain, and the central nervous system of the planet, then the planetary being is coming to consciousness of itself, reflected through human consciousness. And if we try to destroy that human consciousness, we're actually aborting the process of planetary life.

There's no question that the great gift of art has been to heighten, foster, and encourage individuality. Artists are loners. They work better in civilizations than they work in communities. Communities tend to be a little crushing on them. So Yeats, or Wordsworth, or Michelangelo became part of the civilization we call Europe. Even in Ireland the Irish revolutionaries didn't like Yeats, because he didn't write propaganda, and he wasn't only pro-Ireland. He was helping Ireland become conscious of itself, so that Ireland could make its contribution to Europe. So Yeats was really a member of the wider community of Europe. Small communities tend to be threatened by people of a different orientation. And so, traditionally, artists have had to back off and say, "Hey, I'll make a contribution, but give me space to make it. I can't belong to your commune or your village; I need space to do my own thing."

So, the dominant image of the artist today is really the artist of the second phase that you described.

Since the Renaissance and Modernism, it's been individuation, the artist as hero.

Yes. The artist as a super-individual, as an authority. What about the image of the artist of the third phase?

I think it turns on a spiral and takes a bit from the more anonymous folk stage. One of the characteristics of, say, the matrilineal village unit is the lack of private property and names. So you don't have fame. All children are equally the children of the Great Mother. The anonymous artist might want to go back to the collective creativity in which the Great Mother was honored in a cathedral like Chartres, for example. The cathedrals would be signed, "Adamo me fecit."

At the same time, we're obviously not going to go back to complete anonymity. There have been some really nice artists, like the sculptor Harold Tovish at MIT, who is a totally unpretentious man who is disgusted and turned off by the histrionics of an Andy Warhol and the kind of "public relations manager" approach to being the artist, always being seen with the beautiful people. Tovish longed for anonymous art. And there is a man in Zurich who did some "graffiti" on many of the concrete buildings in that city. His calligraphy was like Kandinsky's; it was so good and witty that he became famous. Eventually they found him, and the police put him in jail for defacing public buildings. All the art community of Zurich came to his rescue saying, "No, this is spontaneous, conceptual art!" But before he was caught, he always worked anonymously. Yet, even he ended up in the newspaper. And even Harold Tovish has a name. So I think once you're out of the womb of the Great Mother, and you're in the sunlight, you can't really go back to the darkness of anonymity.

What artists are struggling with now is how to be creative without all the trappings of the Wagnerian ego. The Wagnerian artist is really a pathology, the stage of individuation taken to its extreme. Once an artist is individuated, he does not need to scream "I am here!" The Wagnerian phase is one of domination where the artist says, "I am more important than you. I am more important than nature. I am the most important thing." That, obviously, is a pathological response.

I think a lot of artists are saying, "How can I belong to a moral order? Well, I'd like to have an association with something like the ETA Project, but I'd want to do it on my terms. I don't want to get into something like 'New Age Art' because that's kind of kitsch, and I don't want to get into religious art because that's kind of self-deluding. Yet I don't want to just be into the narcissism of the marketplace of New York." It's very hard for them to find the balance; it's no easy thing. But I think it will have to be done.

There are examples of artists who have played a healthy role in helping society come to consciousness of itself. Yeats, for example, was definitely a man of his time. He was the last of the romantics and wore his flowing silk tie, and flowing hair, and had a dandyish way about him that was very off-putting, especially to working-class people. He had a certain kind of aristocratic posturing and was fairly conservative politically, though he helped the Irish Revolution as a senator in Ireland. But he aided the movement of Irish liberation and individuation most by helping Ireland become conscious of itself.

Today the vehicle of cultural change is not nationalism. That's been done; we've been working on that for a couple of centuries. The artist is trying to help the human race become conscious of itself as a planetary culture, so artists have to form associations the way

Yeats founded the Abbey Theatre—not to foster revolutionary nationalism, but to foster planetary culture. Therefore, works that can bring people together and make them conscious of their involvement in one another become very important.

The mass arts are extremely important here, even if some of it is really kind of ugly and violent and a reflection of the destructiveness of our media-controlled society. Some aspects of Punk, and New Wave, and popular art forms, and music video are very important forms of global communication. They're coming out of England, but they're influencing California, and New York, and Europe and working their way down into Latin America and even into the Soviet Union. Some Punks—Boy George and Culture Club, for example, are really a fairly sophisticated way of recycling the working class. They've said, "Okay, here we are on the dole. Nobody needs us. They don't need us as working class in factories; they don't need us as serfs on the great estates in Russia; and they don't need us as slaves, as they once used us in the Roman Empire. They have no need for us at all." They've taken their dole, and they've created a whole industry of music video and popular music and created these global forms of communication. So they have, in a sense, created art styles out of new forms of nationalism.

Take the Turks in Germany, a working class that is hated by racists in Germany. They were brought in to make Volkswagens and now, because there is unemployment, the Germans want to ship them back to Turkey. But if these Turks would draw upon Middle Eastern sources of music and create a new form of popular music that could influence Europe and North America, then they would begin to gain recognition, and freedom, and respect the way the Blacks did in the United States. If you trace the rise of the Blacks here to the point where Jesse Jackson can run for President of the United States and not be considered a joke, you find it is directly related to the rise of Dixieland, and Jazz, and then Rock and Roll. With each phase, from around the late 1890's to now, music helped speak to the Whites, and people like Duke Ellington became figures of cultural respect and integration. So the role of music, in terms of fostering racial harmony, is not to be underestimated at all.

If Maggie Thatcher were smart, she would see that the dole is really a form of investment in the working class with which they imaginatively create a whole new enterprise that hires millions of people and creates a mammoth industry. And actually, the dole that is spent in England on the working class—these punk kids that hang around the King's Road in Chelsea—is far less than was spent on the Concorde or nuclear reactors. So in terms of cost-effectiveness, the return on investment is really fantastic, and Maggie Thatcher is just looking at it the wrong way.

Having made that point, do you see any promising trends in "high" art?

Yes. I think we can work our way up in exactly the way we did in the romantic period, folk music having inspired serious composers and poets such as Bartok, Wordsworth, and Yeats. We start with rock music and move into transitional figures like Laurie Anderson, for example. She can be called "pop" and can be seen in the rock genre as analagous to David Bowie, and at the same time she really appeals to the intelligentsia and moves toward the music of opera, such as that of Philip Glass. His score for the film *Koyaanisquatsi*, or his opera, *Satyagraha*, are "high" art. He seems to me very much the kind of artist who is sensitive to this new culture and understands it. And his music is, I think, quite beautiful.

What about film?

Film is a highly successful, culture-shaping art form that has integrated European and North American cultures. But in terms of breakthrough, the cutting edge for me is in that intensely tight, compact form of music video animation and video synthesizers. You can take very complex ideas and give visual analogues for them and actually, in some computers, you can present four and five-dimensional models on a two-dimensional surface. You can't do that on a blackboard with chalk!

How does all of this relate to the third phase of history that you spoke of earlier? I am particularly interested in the degree to which you think these artists are conscious of the larger picture. Do they intuitively dig it up? Is it unconscious? To what degree can this kind of art be conscious?

Some of it depends on the biological accident of the intelligence of the artist. There are many artists who don't have to be intelligent to work effectively; they are skilled or they are very intuitive. The really gigantic artists who effect the unfoldment of civilization—like Shakespeare or Goethe or Dante—understand what they are doing because they combine, in a powerful way, an enormous sensitivity to the unconscious, and a tremendously developed intuitition and sensitivity to the superconscious, with a highly developed intelligence. So they're in a class apart. People like Ronald Reagan or Boy George are collective representations that are thrown up by the culture; they are not highly conscious, only reflective of the mass mind. There is no question, for example, that Philip Glass knows what he's doing in his opera *Satyagraha*. He has a vision of culture, and visions of war and peace, and human dignity, and human rights, and racism, and they are wed to a theory of music.

Now, some artists are so dominated by their message that they become propagandistic, and those artists generally appeal only to people who are members of the cult. If you've got a message, take it to Western Union. Art is not message. The only people who care about Soviet socialist realism are commissars in the Soviet Union. Even the Russians themselves don't take that stuff seriously anymore. And there are people in Auroville who think that Sri Aurobindo's *Savitri* is the greatest work of art the world has ever seen. But anybody who is a poet or is knowledgeable about poetry can barely finish reading the work. It's the usual "devotee" syndrome; that's just human nature. It only bothers me when we are surrounded by devotees who are trying to convince us that the poetry of Kahlil Gibran or Paramahansa Yogananda or Sri Aurobindo or Gopi Krishna is really great art. It's not to be taken any more seriously than Soviet socialist realism.

What do you think is the practice of the artist? What goes into creating good art?

Well, it all happens on several levels at once, like the musical score of a Bach fugue. The first level is the celebrative level. Art is, in the creative process itself, a celebration of thanksgiving to God for the gift of being. We're said to be made in the image and likeness of God, and we see God only in the expression of His handiwork in the Universe and His signature in the crystals of the snowflake or the turns of the spiral nebulae. So the way in which we are like God, can imitate Him, and can show our close relationship to Him, is in the creative process itself. Art is an act of intimacy because it comes out of one's own interiority and is addressed to the interiorness of things in the Universe.

Another level of the artistic process is the integrative aspect of art.

It is a way of attuning and aligning ego with the higher self, the daimon, and it provides self-knowledge: remembrance of past lives, or repressed childhood experiences and traumas, or new insights about self and the world. And as a personal voyage of self-discovery, it helps make one more of a whole being.

The next level is the associative. Once you understand yourself and can have compassion for yourself, then you are in a better position to have compassion for others. You can reach out to your fellow human beings and communicate with them. What you're doing is giving thanks to your fellow human beings for the gift of the language, or culture, or tradition in which you live. So, as a writer in the English language, I'm having an extended conversation with Yeats and Shakespeare, even though I may never be as good as Yeats or Shakespeare. It is a way of recognizing that I couldn't become as conscious of myself and my fellow human beings if they hadn't created this literature in the English language. Therefore, I'm reaching out and associating with them.

If my roots are deep in the past, and I'm not just superficially dealing with the trends of the moment, and if I'm aware of the sources reaching all the way back to the birth of the English language—to Anglo-Saxon and Celtic influences or, maybe even deeper into world literature, through the Greek and Roman and back to the Gilgamesh Epic in ancient Egypt and in Asia as well— if I'm deeply rooted in that, then I can more effectively reach out to associate with my fellow human beings and say, "Now I would like to give thanks for the gift that has been given to me, that has made my life so rich, by trying to create a work of art that will be a return of the energy and a thanks to the civilization or a thanks to the human race." So in that sense, the social aspect is very much a recapitulation of the celebrative, of giving thanks to God in the privacy of the creative process.

Sometimes the artist will be so far in anticipation of the future of the race that the present can't accept it. So someone like William Blake, for example, really didn't come into his own until the very late nineteenth century when Yeats rediscovered him. Even Bach was really rediscovered by Mendelssohn. So sometimes there's a lag. If artists are lucky, they can bring all three of those levels together: celebrating God, giving consciousness to their historical moment and making their society more conscious of itself, and discovering the dimensions of their own personal being in the creative act. Shakespeare, certainly, was able to do that and was revered in his own time, honored by Queen Elizabeth. Bach never really got the recognition that he deserved, though he wasn't totally ignored.

Yeats really consummated the romantic era, helped bring a nation into being, helped to dismember a technologically oppressive empire and made a contribution to the mind of Europe and Western civilization. He was revered in his own time and he won the Nobel Prize. That doesn't always happen. Joyce didn't get the Nobel Prize, and he died in exile under unhappy circumstances. Sometimes the artist is more like the *Pietà* of Michelangelo, in which the artist is the victim. Sometimes artists like this role and bring it upon themselves.

How much does that archetype of suffering hold artists?

Some artists are afraid of success because they feel it will make them sell out and lose their "perfectness." So they invoke failure to ensure their perfection or their virginity. Others lust after the apotheosis of martyrdom, and want to be victimized. It's a pathological neurosis. But artists are people, so they can be neurotic.

You mentioned three levels of the artistic process. Are there others?

I think I described them in historical succession: first is prayer—silence, invocation, the blank page looking up at you; then comes the voyage of self-discovery, followed by the association with a tradition. The fourth, I guess, is performance, the public life of the artist. The book is published; it's no longer yours; it's now gone out into the world and, if it's a good work, it may help other people prayerfully attune to God, discover things about themselves, and relate to their society. So the fourth level is the unitary level of the three in which society begins to participate through the public performance of the work.

So, at its best, art is given as a gift to people.

Art is nothing if not public. Even a poem that's written in solitude is written in the English language, and that's not a private act. It would only be private if I invented my own language.

Literally, in Latin, "perform" means "through form." So an intent, an inspiration, is squeezed through form. What I'm missing in your

*description of these four levels is the issue of crafting, which
insures that the form is true.*

I see that as part of what I call the "associative" stage. When
working with the English language, you are relating to traditions of
excellence. I spoke of Shakespeare and Yeats because so much of the
quality of what makes a poem great and what is required for
language—not just self-therapy or self-expression—is associated
with the standards of excellence. So there is a craft of poetry that is
quite demanding, and there is a craft to sculpture, and weaving,
and music. Our culture has a concern for excellence; it has simply
misplaced it. Our airplanes, for example, are rather pretty and have
to be made with immaculate attention to detail, or everybody in
them can get killed. The computer is pretty meticulously put
together. But in their personal lives, people don't have the level of
skill or craft that a folk society might have, for example.

*Do you think that these four phases of artistic practice are relevant
to people who are not artists, like business people?*

Ideally, the businessperson should be thinking, "I am part of a
service; I am actually trying to facilitate the culture and help people
do and create." The people who make the Apple computer presum-
ably are doing it not just to become millionaires, but to change the
culture and allow people to do different kinds of work. Scientists
certainly use the celebrative level—the Einsteins and the Faradays
and the Heisenbergs and others—and move then to self-discovery.
Sciences are a form of self-discovery as well, and good scientists are
very intuitive. And at the associative level, they're in dialogue with
Newton, and Einstein, and all the great scientists back to Pythag-
oras. The performance of their work is its testing in the laboratory,
where it begins to be part of civilization.

*I feel that art needs to spill from museums and concert halls into
the roads and the cities? Do you agree?*

Well, that happens. Take the Centre Pompideau in Paris. The
street life outside the Centre Pompideau in some ways is more
interesting than the inside. There are jugglers, and performers, and
street musicians, and there is Tinguely Fountain. So it's a work of
art that's sort of mediating between the stuff inside the museum
and the public space outside. It's vibrant with life. The Centre

Pompideau has totally transformed and energized the Les Halles part of Paris.

Museums are really a way of recycling the culture. They were originally houses of aristocrats or kings—like the Louvre—and then were turned into culture boxes for the acquisitive upper-middle class who went around ripping off the cultures of the world and stuffing the art into boxes. Then the poor working class, on the open free days after church, got to wander through and get an education. So for a poor kid like myself, going through a museum was an attempt to reach out to a world that was larger than my normal range of experience. I've always taken my kids to museums like the MOMA or the Met, and I've always liked the way that they inspire and vivify the street life.

The return of street musicians is a recent phenomenon. There was a period of urban sterility which was, I think, kind of a post-Le Corbusier period of the city-as-the-machine-for-living, in which the spaces were all sterile, quantitative, and vacant. The ideal in the fifties was the shopping plaza. My first awareness of an alternative came with Ghiradelli Square in San Francisco, which is an old factory reconverted into a public consortium of boutiques, bookstores, restaurants, coffee shops, and ice cream parlors. The street musicians turned it into a performance space with enormous success.

There was a crisis in Bern when the orderly Swiss wanted to clean the streets of ruffians and vagabonds, tinkers and musicians. The head of the Conservatory of Music said, "No!" and came out onto the street and started playing the piano, saying that this was part of city life and should not be against the law. He was able to talk the city council of Bern into passing an ordinance that this be tolerated, although the musicians could play for half an hour only before moving to a different spot. Now Bern is alive with all kinds of very good music from all over the world. So I think museums are just an historical scrapbook of the family of humanity.

I know that you just finished writing a novel. Can you say a bit about it?

I wasn't planning a novel; it just exploded in my head, and I became possessed and taken over by this book. It came out of nowhere; I was totally surprised. It took me over entirely so that, in a two-month period, I wrote something like four hundred pages, which is a good clip, and rewrote, and rewrote, and found myself breaking down, and crying, and having intense memories of the distant past. It was like going through a psychoanalytic clearing out.

Everything I've ever written has been about myth and history and the ambiguous relationship between the two. I've always moved out into the "twilight zone," the edge where history ends and myth begins, and in that kind of penumbral darkness, one can't quite make out whether these Pythagorases, or King Arthurs, or Quetzalcoatls are imaginary or real . . . .

Those interested in knowing more about William Irwin Thompson's work, contact The Lindisfarne Association, Cathedral Church of St. John the Divine, 1047 Amsterdam Avenue, New York, NY 10025.

Philip Glass

Philip Glass, the American composer, has become a preeminent figure on the international music scene, writing for opera, film, theater, dance, chorus, and for his own group, the *Philip Glass Ensemble.* A graduate of the Julliard School, Mr. Glass has received numerous commissions and awards, including a Fulbright Scholarship, which enabled him to study with Nadia Boulanger in Paris. He is a CBS Masterworks recording artist, the first composer to be offered this distinguished contract since Aaron Copland. *Glassworks* was his first Masterworks release, followed by *The Photographer, Einstein on the Beach* and, in May of 1985, *Satyagraha.* Mr. Glass wrote the score for the Peter Weir film, *Koyaanisqatsi,* and for Paul Schrader's film, *Mishima,* which won the Best Musical Achievement award at the 1985 Cannes film festival. He also composed the music for the opening and closing ceremonies of the 1984 Summer Olympics held in Los Angeles.

Glassworks *was my introduction to Philip Glass' work. I found the music very beautiful, filled with layer upon layer of dynamic progression, creating images of the play of light on the surface of water and the deep slow currents below. In following his work, I became intrigued by his choice of subject matter for opera: Einstein, Gandhi, Akhnaten. A friend arranged for me to meet Mr. Glass, and the following interview took place in his home in New York City in June of 1984.*

*   *   *

How do you perceive the current cultural context in which you work?

I tend to work as internationally as I can—in Western Europe, Japan, and North America. I discovered that there wasn't enough work in America alone. I do tours—one in Europe every year, one in America with the ensemble—and operas that are written more for European audiences than American.

Is the prime motivation for your international work economic, or is there a deeper reason also?

I would have to say that the prime motivation is economic. The first problem that an artist has is how to survive; I have no means of support apart from my work. Had I taken an academic route, I would have had economic security. My goal has always been to support myself from the work that I do—work that I choose to do, not work that responds to a commercial marketplace. I began writing music when I was fifteen and was not self-supporting as an artist until I was forty-one. So for over twenty-five years, I could not entirely support myself through the work that I wanted to do. The struggle to reach a point where my entire efforts could be put into music was important, and it was important that I do it under conditions that were acceptable to me. That meant I had to do it independently, adhering closely to an artistic vision that seemed authentic.

Can you say more about that vision?

Well, that is the hardest thing to talk about. I can talk more easily about all the other things. The struggle to develop an artistic language, a voice, is a very personal one. That is a problem that artists have always had.

*It seems that over the past century an increasing trend in artistic
work has been toward making a "name" for oneself. In some cases
that has led artists to very personal, even self-centered, and
sometimes very esoteric expressions. Another possibility is that
artists be more relevant to their cultures and times and have some
sense of what needs exist in society in order to serve them. How do
you approach this?*

For many years the work that I did had no large public. I really
wasn't that well known. So what were my reasons for writing
music? I can't honestly say that I was serving the needs of society; it
never occurred to me. I was simply interested in writing music.

When I was thirty-two, I found myself with a showcase for the
work that I was doing, and a language that, in retrospect, seems
primitive in some ways, but was adequate to serve my artistic needs
at that time. I wrote pieces then that I cannot improve on now
without totally re-conceiving them. At that point, I reached the first
level of what I consider to be a functioning artist: I knew that my
best work was ahead of me, but I knew that I was no longer
struggling for a voice. It took another ten years before there was an
economic match to that artistic situation.

Then my struggle became one of surviving in order to do the work
that I wanted to do. It happened that from a very early point, there
was a small audience that was appreciative of my work. It centered
in the community of artists that lived in downtown New York—
theater and visual artists, dancers, some musicians. This was a real
context for my music. Now, over the years, I have expanded way
beyond that original audience. But it wasn't until I began working
on large theater pieces that the larger audience became essential.

You see, you can rarely separate economic motivations from
artistic ones. At the point where you begin to do large theater works,
which only repertory opera companies can do, requiring maybe
two-hundred persons to stage, six weeks to rehearse, and three or
four months to design, you're talking very big-scale pieces. You
cannot do big-scale pieces for audiences of fifty or sixty, the size I
originally played for. It simply is not viable; no one would produce
the work. Had I decided to remain with the ensemble alone, I could
have continued playing for fifty or sixty people forever. It is a
completely satisfying relationship from a composer's point of view. If
you have fifty or a hundred or two-hundred people who love the
work, what's the difference? It's only a decimal point away from

65

two-thousand. And it doesn't qualitatively make it any better to have a bigger audience. The satisfaction that an artist feels can be gained very quickly from an authentic audience relationship.

So, society at large became important when I began to do big-scale pieces, which became large social events; a work for the Stuttgart Opera becomes something that everyone in that town knows about. After fifteen performances a year over a period of several years, I would say that there isn't a person in that city who doesn't know an opera has taken place.

The image you project is that of an artist who is very much at the influence and mercy of trends. What are some other influences?

You have to remember that I helped to shape those trends, that the musical life of the city that I live and work in is very different now from seventeen or eighteen years ago. I am one of the people who made that happen.

Who, in your mind, are some others?

Well, there are many: the Living Theater, Mabou Mines Theater Collective, with whom I worked for many years, Meredith Monk, and Bob Wilson, and sculptors like Richard Serra—people who create artistic values that become the recognizable culture of the time. You can say that we're at the mercy of it all, but we are also the creators of it. Our relationship to society is always complex.

Now, I know what you're driving at, and eventually I'll get to it, but I think it is very important to see the social context that the artist works in. My work was originally completely unacceptable to the music world that I was living in. At this point, it is not only totally acceptable, but I am now seen by some younger composers as though I had always been alive and working. In fact, the difference between an opera director who would refuse to listen to a tape five years ago and who now may be anxious to produce my work is very impressive.

That must be very satisfying to you.

To be satisfied is hardly the point; it is just the way it works. To take pleasure in that would be to rob it of the fatalism that it has. Do you see what I mean? It's not a personal issue; it's the way the world works. You can look at Berlioz and say the same thing. I'm not comparing my work to his, but looking at it from a social point of view, it's a struggle that anyone has in coming from being seen as a radical figure to being identified as a person who creates the culture of the times and, finally, to being considered as one of the icons. I'm too young for that, and I don't know whether it will ever happen. But it's a mechanism; to say that *I* did it is to place myself in a position of power which I don't have.

But you want to talk about my real motivation for writing music. I don't separate these issues, because every day that I work, I come back to that point.

What is that point?

It's the point where I am alone with music. This is, I would say, the fundamental relationship. The reason I talk about these other things is that in this society . . . . Where are you from?

I was born in Yugoslavia.

I do not know how it is there, but I have to tell you that this society, in relationship to artists, is one of the most brutal societies that you can imagine. There are other classes who are also treated very badly—old people, for example, or people who don't speak English well. You're safe by the color of your skin, but had you the wrong skin color *and* the accent, you'd be in trouble. We have a fairly narrow spectrum of "safe" groups of people in this country. Artists definitely are outside of that safe spectrum.

I don't know any artists—and I've talked to many—whose parents asked them to become artists. I don't know of any who didn't on their own say, "I'm going to be a painter," or "I'm going to be a sculptor." Then later on, when artists say, "I'm not doing well; I'm having a hard time," people respond, "Who asked you to do it?" or "If you want to spend time painting pictures, that's fine, but don't expect *us* to help you." This is the American life; this is the way we do it here.

That's why these questions come up. But we come back to why, in the face of this, one will do it anyway? American artists are among the strongest in the world. For reasons that are not clear—maybe the heterogeneous nature of the society, or the extreme independence of the artist in learning to survive, or maybe the lack of real tradition in the arts in this country—we develop very strong artistic personalities. To begin as an artist means to take on a life of struggle, so that at forty-one you can finally make a living as an artist. My European artist friends would say, "My gosh, it took you so long!" But in this country you'd say, "You mean you did it so quickly?" It can just as easily never happen.

Music is one of the few places that I know of where the meeting of our intellectual life and our emotional life takes place; the possibility of forming a perfect match can take place through music. We can use our brains and at the same time respond. The raw stuff of art becomes emotions which are captured through this strange and elaborate process of artistic technique. It's a very curious phenomenon. I think when one is struck by it, it can become the focus of all one's energy. In this way, being an artist is more like a vocation; it's a calling, in that one can't be asked to do it and also can't be dissuaded from doing it. It sounds abstract, but it's also a daily process. Working every day at it makes it very immediate and totally engaging. I think that's a primary motivation.

And there are many others. For some people there are simpler things—like money and power and fame—the usual gamut of human gratification. There are few artists who don't hold some of those desires. But the primary one for me is that one area where a most intangible thing can be made almost as solid as a rock.

To what degree do you think of yourself as taking on a lineage of work?

I think very little about that. I spent two or three years finishing my music studies in Paris and was struck by the enormous difference in the sense of history the European artist has in relation to the American artist. I remember Nadia Boulanger, my teacher, telling me one day, "You know, a great sadness for me is that you Americans have no sense of history." Of course, any American could have told her that having no history can be a great gift and a great opportunity but, in fact, she was exactly right. On the other hand, I feel that the history of music is my history too. Rather, it's my relationship to it that's different, so that if I think of orchestration, I think about Shostakovich, and Mahler, and Berlioz; if I think about vocal writing, I think of Verdi and Monteverdi. They are my history too. I never would have believed that we could be so different had I not lived in Europe and seen that the European artists relate to their traditions so differently from the way that we do.

You're an American, yet you studied in Europe. Maybe the differ-
ence is one of being able, as an American, to unplug yourself from
this culture and explore all the other cultures.

Well, the American identity is fairly recent in terms of cultural
history. What are we talking about—two or three-hundred years?
And it's mostly a hodge-podge. My family is from Russia, but I can't
say that I have any sense of being Russian at all. In fact, we are
Russian Jews, which is different from being Russian. I might have
been Polish, depending on how you drew the map. My girlfriend's
family is part Chinese and part Irish. Going back only two generations, the families of all my close friends are from Europe. I don't
think I know anyone whose ancestors came over on the Mayflower.
The lineage of my Black friends is older in America than mine! You'll
also find that West coast artists grow up looking West more than we
do on the East coast, being closer to Europe, not only geograph-
ically, but emotionally. From the point of view of Belgrade, we are all
Americans; but if you're here, believe me, you can tell the difference.

In terms of the whole climate of the arts in general, we are moving
toward a much more international feel anyway. For example, when I
studied in music school more than twenty-five years ago, there was
no music taught that was not Western music. Any music that was
outside of the Western tradition was considered primitive. This
corresponded exactly to a general attitude of Western culture vis-a-
vis the rest of the world. We were the civilized world, and everyone
else was—now we have a euphemism for it—the "developing world,"
the undeveloped, pre-industrial societies that could make no claim
to sophistication of any kind, including the arts. And this idea was
largely accepted by artists.

The Second World War brought us into much closer contact with
the rest of the world on an international level. So that even things
like guitar players deciding they wanted to play sitar had a tremendous impact on the culture of this country. By the '60s, as John
Cage said in one of his books, America was just another part of the
world, no more and no less, and there were several great traditions
of music. The African, Indian, Balinese, Japanese, and Western
traditions were parallel, none having any claim of superiority over
another. This change is something that has happened in our time.
Lou Harrison is a very fine composer from the West Coast who has
taken a great interest in the music from Bali. I have personally taken
a great interest in music from southern India. There are other

composers who have taken interest in music from Africa. I've heard it said that this is colonization on another level. But it's actually more complicated than that. When I go to India, in fact, I hear that Western music has now become part of the Indian music. The influence is not one way at all.

Do you have a sense of what the end result of all this cross-pollination will be?

People I know in other countries wish to preserve the identity of their own cultures, but they also do not want to be left out of this great cross-culturalization; so there's a conflict. Can you have both? I don't know. Can you have the purity of traditional music and at the same time be open to the traditions of Western repertory opera? I don't know. It's very hard to say whether the results will be good or bad. Probably they'll be both.

Take someone like Satyajit Ray from Calcutta, a filmmaker who clearly understands the history of film. This is a Western art form, and he is a master filmmaker working in a medium that is not Indian. There are novelists who come from non-Western countries, working in the tradition of the novel, which didn't exist in those countries before. And I've been enriched by traditions that I came across in my travels, first in Europe, then North Africa, then central Asia and India. The curious thing for me is that I am told my music sounds very American. And not only that, but people in Europe will say, "Your music is from New York." And people from New York even know what part of town it is from. My predeliction has been to participate in an aesthetic understanding of other traditions as much as I could. The way that has been incorporated is personal to the point that it's not apparent, yet I could not be writing the music I'm writing today had I not traveled widely.

You mentioned earlier that music provides a synthesis between the intellect and the emotions. Where does the spiritual side fit into your music? Your operas explore things like the life of Gandhi and the Egyptian mysteries. What compels you to write about these things more than, say, the life of President Eisenhower?

I recently read a quote from *The Brothers Karamazov*, by Dostoyevsky, about the mystery of beauty. It's a very striking passage about God setting a terrible mystery for man to unravel which we'll never figure out. I prefer to leave these questions out of my speculations. It's enough simply to master a technique, or even master economic survival, or to grasp some real idea of how our culture interacts with others to form something which becomes the life of the late twentieth century. We're beginning to see something which could not be described as simply French, or American, or Bulgarian, or Russian, or Iranian, or anything. So there is something peculiar to this moment in history, and these are the questions that I think about.

Spiritual things—my God—I can't even begin to think of. I don't think I'm smart enough to do that. There are people who do, like Thomas Merton, or the Dalai Lama, but they're specialists just like the rest of us.

Yesterday I met with Paul Winter, a musician who incorporates the sounds of animals, like whales or wolves, into his music. He's concerned about ecological issues and the survival of the earth, and in some ways he's saying, "My music will be a vehicle through which I express that concern." Do you have a similar dialogue going on?

No, I don't. I have a more fatalistic attitude.

How's that?

Well, there are two answers to that question. For the most part I tend to deny it but, in fact, if I look at the work that I do, I have to admit that there seems to be some underlying interest . . . . There's a work about Gandhi one about Einstein, one about Akhnaten, who again was one of the watersheds in the development of human consciousness. The next major work that I'm doing is based on a book by Doris Lessing, *The Making of the Representative for Planet Eight.* It's the story of a whole planet that is freezing to death; the whole planet's dying.

Now why did you choose that among so many wonderful stories?

The questions she raises in the book are among the most interesting I can think of. Without giving away the story, *The Making of the Representative* is about how we face the possibility of not surviving. How do we face the possibility that no one is going to come and save us? The planet is dying; there's been an ecological disaster; all heat has left the planet; the planet has moved out of its course. The people have been assured by their neighboring planet that they are going to be taken away and all will be safe, and at some point they realize that their helpers are not going to come, that they're going to be left to deal with it all by themselves. What could be more the question of today? This is the most interesting work I can do right now. On the one hand, my overt intentions are really not to polemicize; I don't get ideological in that way; I stay away from that. But, in fact, the work that I have done in the last nine years is all about questions of this kind. So I must say that, in spite of myself, or in truth to myself, I'm doing it anyway.

It takes two or three years to write an opera. I have to take on something that's going to last me that long, that will carry me through. The works that interest me are those that touch on fundamental issues, so that's what I end up doing. Apart from the work itself, I rarely talk about these issues. I never discuss my anxieties about the future of mankind. I don't take part in panels on ecology. But, on the truest level of my work, I can't deny that this seems to be the sort of thing that I do. I find myself unwilling to talk about it. Yet, I am unable to work in any other way.

Do you think that you're typical in that sense, that by necessity artists, if they're really sensitive to what's going on in their world, must really consider these issues?

Most of the artists that I know in some way or another deal with these problems. There are a few who work in some kind of abstract aesthetic, whose work I admire, and whose work doesn't seem to be socially conscious in that way. But in the theater arts, where I spend a lot of my time, I find that many artists are conscious of these issues now, more perhaps than in the past. It's hard to say. I don't know what it was like to experience society fifty years ago; I've no way to know that. Rarely will someone admit to not being concerned about these things. It would be interesting if someone did; it would be an interesting point of view.

The reason your name caught my attention was precisely by your choice of subject matter. It seems that you are consistently dancing around some issue.

Who is it that said that we ooze self-betrayal? No matter what I say, or what appears in your book, or what I may say in another interview about this or that, if you look at the body of my work, it points in a certain direction. My reluctance to speak about it may be that I have almost nothing to say outside the work itself. I have much more to say about the economic situation of the artist or the social situation of the artist. Those are easy things to talk about. But the larger issue of the fate of the world, I mean, my God! I find that an unthinkable question.

Are you ever afraid of what might happen?

I tell you, fear doesn't enter into it. It's too abstract an idea. I can't imagine the world not existing, so I have no fear of it not existing. On the other hand, I know for a fact that there are enough maniacs around capable of blowing the world up. But even as I say it, part of me doesn't believe it's possible. Isn't this the comfort that we all live in?

Where do you do most of your work?

I found a place in Nova Scotia, in Canada, far away from everyone, and I spend a month there at a time. It's a fairly raw state of nature. I have a cabin in the woods which got electricity only very recently. The nearest house is a few hundred yards away. I usually work with the door open—weather permitting—sitting on the step outside the cabin and looking at the trees. I must spend half my time looking outside and the other half writing.

There must be quite a contrast between your cabin and the house here on this busy and noisy corner of the East Village.

You can't believe what a contrast it is! To come back to New York is always shocking. I never get over it.

You must like New York.

Well, I made my peace with it certainly. Also, I thrive on the stimulation, and not just artistic stimulation, but the stimulation of people and events. This neighborhood is a particularly lively one, and I've chosen to live here for the last fifteen years. All kinds of things happen here which I find very interesting and very peculiar.

Last night there was a blind man walking down the street. He had glasses, frames with no lenses. And he came across another vagrant sitting on a box and hit this person with his cane. Then he broke the cane against the fence with a cry of complete rage and yelled, "Where's my stick?" It was the strangest bit I've ever seen. The man sitting on the box was half-naked. His pants were down to his knees. The blind man couldn't find the other end of his cane, and the half-naked man couldn't get up, not because he was half-naked, but because he hadn't moved all day. I mean, you couldn't have written a stranger scene than this. That's very different from sitting and looking at trees.

Somebody else might walk by and not pay any attention.

I notice it all the time. The "human comedy," our life as we know it. I find it very interesting.

Your music revolves around repetition of a certain theme. Why is that?

Why did that language develop? Well, there are musical reasons for that. The period of music I grew up in was dominated by an avant-garde attitude about music which had to do with technique that was originally European-based. The important composers then were people like Stockhausen and, in this country, Carter or Kirshner. As a young man, this was not the kind of music that was attractive to me. So I had to find a different language to work in, and I took a very extreme position, a kind of opposition to this very evolved technique, by reducing all the music that I knew to something based on the simplest materials I could think of.

Also, one of my main interests was the idea of rhythmic structure in music. Almost any music that is non-Western uses rhythmic structure. It sounds like an over-simplification, but it's consistently true. I saw this rhythmic structure as a powerful technique that I could make into a personal vocabulary. Many of these rhythmic structures are repetitive, and in the beginning I worked with very simple tonal relationships through a very slow evolution of material. It's developed a lot since 1965, but it is still recognizable in the music even now.

Sometimes the effect can be very hypnotic. Is that what you want to achieve?

As a matter of fact, it doesn't affect me that way at all; my experience of it makes me very awake. When I was young, I heard a performance of Beethoven's *Ninth* and saw people sleeping in the audience. So what can I tell you? Some people wake up, and some go to sleep, whether it's Beethoven or whoever.

What would you like your audience to experience?

First of all, I would like them to have the same experience of music that I have. Of course, that is not achievable. When I write the music, I hear the language of music as the most powerful way of achieving a specific response that will affect me in a certain way. But I'm aware that other people hear very differently, so I long ago gave up the idea that they would hear it the way I do. On the other hand, there's enough similarity in the way they hear, it seems, that a consensus in an audience can take place. In *Satyagraha*, which is the opera about the early life of Mahatma Gandhi, the very last thing that's sung uses words that come from the Bhagavad-Gita about how, in every age, a hero is born to carry on the fight of good against evil. It's a very simple idea, and the music at that moment is my response to the text; it merges with the text in a way that makes a statement about it. It seems that other people hear it that way as well, though I suppose some hear it as trivial or as boring. But enough people hear it as uplifting so that it's a very special moment at the end of the opera. I've seen it performed many times and with many audiences, and I can feel the audience having contact with the music and text in a way that seems very consistent and appropriate to the material.

But the first listener is myself; for any artist this is true. For the painter, the first viewer is self; for the poet, the first listener is self. If one is lucky, it can be generally shared. There are some great works that are difficult to communicate and that don't have a large audience. That doesn't make them less wonderful. There are great works of literature which I can't read; they're too difficult for me. I've never succeeded in reading *Ulysses*, for example, though I'm told it's a wonderful piece of literature. I don't doubt it; I simply have never been able to read it. There are works that are difficult, and that does not make them less true.

The artist is a lucky one when the work communicates and is accessible, because it means that things happen, like someone coming to you on the street and saying, "Your music is very important to me," or "I heard your concert, and I was very moved." It's an ancillary result of the work, but one that no artist can fail to appreciate.

Do you ever concern yourself with invoking images of the future?

I'm working on a film biography which will be released in the spring of '85. That's the future for me. Those are the things that I know. I have no fantasies beyond that. You'd be amazed about how little I speculate about the future.

What about the larger future of the world?

Even less. I'm free of fantasies about the future. I'm truly free of them, nor did I have to conquer them. They don't come to me easily, and I never develop them or try to evolve them. I have a very short-term view of the future, which is usually very, very specific— where we're going to eat dinner tonight, who will conduct this work next fall, when the tour to Europe will be. . . .

Sir George Trevelyan

Sir George Trevelyan is widely known in Britain as a lecturer on the spiritual awakening of our time. He was, for twenty-four years, the Principal of Attingham Park, the Shropshire Adult College in Britain, where he experimented with weekend seminars on the holistic and spiritual world-view. After retirement in 1971, he founded the Wrekin Trust, an educational charity concerned with the spiritual nature of humanity and the universe. He is the author of *A Vision of the Aquarian Age* and *Operation Redemption*, as well as the editor of *Magic Casements*, an anthology of poetry expressing the holistic vision which he uses in his lectures to awaken the imaginative faculties.

*In April, 1983, Sir George and I were among the speakers at a
conference at the Findhorn Community in Scotland. Sir George's
love for the Living Word is nowhere as evident as in the passionate
and eloquent speeches in which his topics and identity merge into
a most wonderful whole. After a cozy afternoon tea party we
joined in the following conversation. Alas, his resonant voice,
pregnant pauses, and dignified presence can only be imagined by
the reader.*

*   *   *

*How do you see the arts in relationship to spirituality? What can
the arts do that other areas of our lives, such as politics or
economics, cannot do?*

In our whole movement of spiritual awakening, it is of paramount
importance to recognize the place of the arts. We are experiencing
an evolutionary change in consciousness, making the breakthrough
from the limitations of sense-bound self-consciousness into cosmic
consciousness. A sense of separation from nature has developed
acutely in these last centuries of materialistic thinking, resulting in
what has been called "onlooker consciousness," isolating us from
the world and nature and other people. Much art, therefore, has
concerned itself with the expression of ego and personality, rather
than exploration into the Divinity found within all form. Now, on a
very broad front, an expansion of consciousness seems to be taking
place; the holistic world view is taking over and widening our vision.

It is the same view, of course, that the mystics have always held,
and which has been taught in the mystery traditions of the West,
such as Hermetic philosophy and Rosecrucianism. It involves initiation into the realization that the universe is Mind, not Mechanism,
that man is essentially a being of spirit, soul, and body, that the
entity in us which can say "I" is, in fact, a droplet of Divinity and is
immortal. For this droplet there can be no death, whatever happens
to the body. As this knowledge was lost, we came to think of
ourselves as mere bodies.

So now we are recovering the knowledge that we are really beings
of Spirit, that the universe is a great continuum of living spirit and
divine intelligence, and that this earth is our training ground. We
are here to learn and evolve. In Blake's words: "We are set on earth a
little space, that we may learn to bear the beams of love." We are

learning, as spiritual beings, to operate creatively in freedom. We are
". . . a little lower than the angels and crowned with glory and
honor." This vision is of supreme importance in our death-ridden
culture. It is hard for the cold intellect to grasp it, for it involves a
turn-about in the center of our consciousness. Therefore, the artist
will have a vital task in awakening people to the great truth of man's
immortality and destiny. This great story, this modern myth, can
best be expressed in poetry and drama, painting and sculpture,
dance and ballet, for the arts directly touch the right hemisphere of
the brain. The dormant faculties of vision can be awakened through
the arts.

What we are re-discovering in the holistic world picture is the
meaning of human life on the planet. The spirit of man has come
down from that world of Light into the darkness of separation, and
has the task of finding its higher self, so that it may go back again in
higher consciousness to the plane from which it descended. This is
the experience of initiation. The initiates were filled with absolute
certainty that the soul, the real ego, was immortal. This vision
brings joy and courage in facing the ordeals of life on our plane.

In Greek or Egyptian days, people who revealed the secrets of the
Mysteries were killed; these secrets were simply too powerful for the
"man in the street." So the Mysteries were taught through myths,
the legends and fairy stories that enshroud great spiritual truths.
The myths, in all their diversity, tell one great story: the being of
man which belongs to the eternal world is thrown out of it, falls into
the darkness of Earth, and forgets its divine origin until it finds its
higher self and returns to the world of light. The arts and drama can
teach this great story and so reveal to us our true nature. Art can
become an aspect of redemption.

Can you give an example of this?

Here is a very short fairy story which contains the essential
symbols:

A princess lived in a beautiful palace. Her cruel father threw her
out, and she had to go out into the dark forest. She took with her, as
luggage, three walnut shells, each containing a robe: one was made
of the light of the moon, another made of the light of the stars, and
the third of the light of the sun. Now being lost in the dark night,
she hid herself in a hollow oak. When a huntsman found her and
asked her who she was and where she had come from, she realized

that she had forgotten. So he took her back to his lord's castle where she was put down into the scullery and made to do all the dirty work. Only during the festivals of the year was she allowed to come out, dressed in one of the robes made of the light of the moon, or the light of the stars, or the light of the sun. There she met a prince, who had come from the Higher Realm, who loved and married her, taking her back with him to the land from which she had descended. And (note the finish of a true fairy story) ". . . if they're not dead yet, then they are living still."

The story quite obviously represents the journey of the soul, what Blake called the passage of innocence through experience and on to the New Jerusalem, which he calls Imagination. The princess comes down into the darkness of the forest—symbol of the difficulties of life on this plane—and hides in a hollow tree—symbol surely of the hollow skull (note that the walnut is strangely like the brain, with its convolutions and two hemispheres.) The ego shuts itself in the hollow skull and forgets its name and origin. The Lord of the castle gives her menial work in the scullery. Like the Prodigal Son, she is lost and debased until she comes to herself and says, "I will go back to my Father." With the celestial robes she dances at the festivals of the year, those moments when the heavens are open and contact with Spirit is possible. There the Higher Self meets her, and they recognize each other, and union is established so that she may be led to the New Jerusalem.

That is the story told in ten thousand different myths and tales. The telling of such stories appeals directly to the subconscious. You don't need to intellectualize and analyze it for children, for the soul apprehends its truth. Thus, in a strange way, the telling of fairy stories can be the strongest weapon against dialectical materialism and its total rejection of the Spirit. So much of the technique of transpersonal psychology, the transformational journey, involves our learning to look inward to find our own myths, even to create new ones. The task is to open the eternal worlds, to open the immortal eyes of man inward to the realm of thought, to eternity, ever expanding in the bosom of God. In other words, the gateway to ethereal space is through inner space.

It seems to me that one of the characteristics of this "ethereal" space is that it reveals wholeness to us: we become more aware of how everything is interconnected. It would seem that the emerging sensitivity to ecology and the growing awareness of the holistic viewpoint would also serve as a conscious gateway to this space.

Yes. We are, for instance, becoming aware that this earth on which we tread is alive, really a living organism, a living creature, a part, in turn, of the whole living organism of the solar system. We are not separated from nature; we are the point at which nature and evolution have become consciousness. Humanity also is really a single organism, of which we are all cells, so to speak. We are in the most critical decades of the history of this organism, when we have the potential to become really human or to destroy the whole web of life on the planet. We have taken upon ourselves a god-like responsibility; if we don't wake up very quickly to the fact that we must be responsible stewards of the planet, we are going to be faced with disaster, and it will be very painful.

You are an educator, but you are also an adept of the spoken word, and you have been very successful in your work. Can you say more about that?

I am concerned with the "living word." The doctrine of the living word is, I think, essential for an adult education in spiritual knowledge. To this I would like to add the doctrine of the "living idea," meaning that ideas are truly alive. They are beings, strands of divine intelligence. Plato knew this, and we are now recovering its truth. There is indeed an ethereal plane of living archetypal ideas, which sensitives and initiates can actually see and experience.

In the evolution of consciousness of the last three centuries, and above all of the last century, there has been a powerful development of the intellect. The materialism of our age can be seen as an aspect of the destiny of Western man and the Anglo-Saxon race in particular. Our task has been to grapple with the world of matter and to explore it. In the process, we have developed the left hemisphere of the brain with its critical, analytical, reasoning faculties, and this has enabled us to control and "conquer" nature. The result is our over-masculine, patriarchal culture. The price we have had to pay for that development is the atrophy of the faculties of the right hemisphere of the brain, which are more feminine and sensitive and can apprehend the living whole and the spiritual worlds. These are essentially the artistic and poetic faculties. So the supersensible worlds, the realms of spiritual beings in nature, and the angelic planes have simply disappeared from our awareness, because the faculties for perceiving them have gone dormant. We have lost the poetic faculties of blending with the beings within natural form.

A change in consciousness will involve a re-balancing of the two sides of the brain. Poetry has, for most people, lost its significance, but rightly used it can be a powerful force. For what is a poet but one who is ubiquitous in consciousness, who uses the divine faculty of Imagination. When we truly enter into the spirit and rhythm of a poem, we become one with a tree, a bird, a waterfall, or another person. There is a concept that every species or type of plant or animal has a group ego, an angelic being which is linked with every member of the species by what we call instinct. This being embodies, vivifies, and shapes the idea that has given birth to that species. Thus, one can begin to see that the whole of nature is an expression of a world of living ideas. Within every form of nature is the creative idea, invisible to sense-bound observation and thinking, but apprehended by what Rudolf Steiner called "sense-free thinking." Imagination can apprehend the angelic being and the living idea. As Steiner wrote: "In taking possession of the idea, thinking merges itself into the world mind. What was working without, now works within. Man has become one with the World Being at its highest potency. Such a becoming realized of the idea is the true communion of man."

In reading and reciting poetry, and in learning by heart, it is essential to speak nothing but living thoughts. I refuse absolutely to read dead words. Most people fail lamentably to do this. Live in the thought, allowing the imagination to create images and pictures. As these arise, as if by magic, they can be linked so that one picture will flow into the next. To achieve this, the poem must initially be broken up, taken in slow motion. Live in the images and relish them, allowing a real pause between them. This pregnant pause is the secret. It need not be long, but it must be absolute. In reading or reciting, people must be given time for these images to form. It becomes a lovely and creative process. It is virtually impossible to grasp a poem at one reading, even if well-delivered. This is the illusion that tragically spoils so many poetry recitals.

I find that I must increasingly use poetry in my lectures, because the poet's imagination has created these images, and we, by re-creating, can awaken the pictures and understanding in our own minds. This process activates the dormant faculties of the right hemisphere of the brain. When poetry is used in this way and delivered in a living manner which truly arouses the imagination, people can be moved and lifted. As a teaching aid, it is of primary importance in understanding the spiritual and holistic world view. Thus I feel that use of the living word and the living idea is a craft in its own right.

What advice would you give an artist? What would be the essence to which you would say all artists need to address themselves?

We have spoken of this great myth of the human soul. It is not mere academic theory; it is a vital phenomenon in our dark and brutalized age. While many are filled with doom and gloom, we are filled by a vision of unlimited human potential once we say "yes" to the great Oneness of which we are integrally a part. This spiritual vision can be expressed in the symbols of painting, poetry, sculpture, music, ballet, and architecture. Art can take on a profoundly significant function in the birth of a new age and the re-awakening to the sacred in all life. God is everywhere and manifests through the small voice of our own thinking and in the creative impulse of the heart. To quote Christopher Fry:

> Thank God our time is now
> When wrong comes up to face us everywhere,
> Never to leave us till we take
> The longest stride of soul men ever took.
> Affairs are now soul-size. The enterprise
> Is exploration into God . . . .

Here is the task and inspiration and essential function of art. We can almost prophesy a new renaissance when human consciousness really begins to channel the realm of creative ideas. Signs already show themselves of the birth of holistic art. There is no compulsion and nothing didactic. We are all on the transformational journey looking for the thing that is looking for us. The adventure into art lifts beyond the sometimes dingy attempts to express our personalities and our ego. Such enterprise is exploration into God. Such is the task of art.

Nancy Crompton

Madeleine L'Engle

Madeleine L'Engle's background as an actress, country store-keeper, wife, and mother, provides an excellent variety of materials for her writing, an activity she considers "an essential function, like sleeping and breathing." She wrote her first book, *The Small Rain*, in 1945. Another book, *Meet the Austins*, was written directly out of her experiences as a general store manager in western Connecticut and was named one of the American Library Association's Notable Children's Books of 1960. The author of many fine novels, she is perhaps best known for *The Time Trilogy* fantasy which includes *A Wrinkle in Time*, which brought her the 1963 Newbery Medal for the most distinguished contribution to children's literature, *A Wind in the Door*, and *A Swiftly Tilting Planet*.

Madeleine and I met as co-presenters at a conference given at the Cathedral of Saint John the Divine in New York City. I had read A Wrinkle in Time *and was inspired by her most eloquent synthesis of spiritual sentiments and scientific frontiers, blended into a modern-day story which celebrates human courage. When I approached her with a request for an article or interview for this book, she looked over the paper that described my objectives and told me that she had already addressed the issues in her book,* Walking on Water: Reflections on Faith and Art, *published in 1980, and that she would be happy to contribute selections. Her friend Marilyn Unruh selected the following passages from that book.*

*　　　　　*　　　　　*

I sit on my favorite rock, looking over the brook, to take time away from busy-ness, time to *be*. I've long since stopped feeling guilty about taking *being* time; it's something we all need for our spiritual health, and often we don't take enough of it.

. . .

. . . When I am constantly running there is no time for being. When there is no time for being there is no time for listening. I will never understand the silent dying of the green pie-apple tree if I do not slow down and listen to what the Spirit is telling me, telling me of the death of trees, the death of planets, of people, and what all these deaths mean in the light of love of the Creator who brought them all into being, who brought me into being, and you.

This questioning of the meaning of being, and dying, and being, is behind the telling of stories around tribal fires at night, behind the drawing of animals on the walls of caves, the singing of melodies of love in spring, and of the death of green in autumn. It is part of the deepest longing of the human psyche, a recurrent ache in the hearts of all of God's creatures.

. . .

Not long after I was out of college I read Leo Tolstoy's *What is Art?* and I approached it with reverence and hope. Surely this great writer would provide me with the definitive definition, would show me all the answers. He didn't, and I was naive to expect him to. Generally what is more important than getting water-tight answers is learning to ask the right questions.

. . .

In art, either as creators or participators, we are helped to remember some of the glorious things we have forgotten and some of the terrible things we are asked to endure, we who are children of God by adoption and grace.

In one of his dialogues, Plato talks of all learning as remembering. The chief job of the teacher is to help us to remember all that we have forgotten. This fits in well with Jung's concept of racial memory, his belief that when we are enabled to dip into the intuitive, subconscious self, we remember more than we know. One of the great sorrows which came to human beings when Adam and Eve left the Garden was the loss of memory, memory of all that God's children are meant to be.

. . .

If the work comes to the artist and says, "Here I am, serve me," then the job of the artist, great or small, is to serve. The amount of the artist's talent is not what it is about. Jean Rhys said to an interviewer in the *Paris Review*, "Listen to me. All of writing is a huge lake. There are great rivers that feed the lake, like Tolstoy and Dostoyevsky. And there are mere trickles, like Jean Rhys. All that matters is feeding the lake. I don't matter. The lake matters. You must keep feeding the lake."

To feed the lake is to serve, to be a servant. Servant is another unpopular word, a word we have derided by denigrating servants and service. To serve should be a privilege, and it is to our shame that we tend to think of it as a burden, something to do if you're not fit for anything better or higher.

. . .

When the artist is truly the servant of the work, the work is better than the artist; Shakespeare knew how to listen to his work, and so he often wrote better than he could write; Bach composed more deeply, more truly than he knew; Rembrandt's brush put more of the human spirit on canvas than Rembrandt could comprehend.

When the work takes over, then the artist is enabled to get out of the way, not to interfere. When the work takes over, then the artist listens.

But before he can listen, paradoxically, he must work. Getting out of the way and listening is not something that comes easily, either in art or in prayer.

. . .

Someone wrote, "The principal part of faith is patience," and this applies, too, to art of all disciplines. We must work every day, whether we feel like it or not, otherwise when it comes time to get out of the way and listen to the work, we will not be able to heed it.

~

Stories, no matter how simple, can be vehicles of truth, can be, in fact, icons. It's no coincidence that Jesus taught almost entirely by telling stories, simple stories dealing with the stuff of life familiar to the Jews of his day. Stories are able to help us to become more whole, to become Named. And Naming is one of the impulses behind all art: to give a name to the cosmos we see despite all the chaos.

God asked Adam to name all the animals, which was asking Adam to help in the creation of their wholeness. When we name each other, we are sharing in the joy and privilege of incarnation, and all great works of art are icons of Naming.

When we look at a painting, or hear a symphony, or read a book, and feel more Named, then, for us, that work is a work of Christian art. But to look at a work of art and then to make a judgment as to whether or not it is art, and whether or not it is Christian, is presumptuous. It is something we cannot know in any conclusive way. We can know only if it speaks within our own hearts and leads us to living more deeply with Christ in God.

. . .

The St. Matthew Passion is an icon of the highest quality for me, an open door into the realm of the numinous. Bach, of course, was a man of deep and profound religious faith, a faith which shines through his most secular music. As a matter of fact, the melody of his moving chorale, *O Sacred Head Now Wounded*, was the melody of a popular street song of the day. But Bach's religious genius was so great that it is now recognized as one of the most superb pieces of religious music ever written.

There is nothing so secular that it cannot be sacred, and that is one of the deepest messages of the Incarnation.

~

All children are artists, and it is an indictment of our culture that so many of them lose their creativity, their unfettered imaginations, as they grow older. But they start off without selfconsciousness as they paint their purple flowers, their anatomically impossible people, their thunderous, sulfurous skies. They don't worry that they may not be as good as Di Chirico or Braque; they know intuitively that it is folly to make comparisons, and they go ahead and say what they want to say. What looks like a hat to a grown-up may, to the child artist, be an elephant inside a boa constrictor.

So what happens? Why do we lose our wonderful racketty creativity? What corrupts us?

Corrupt: another unpopular word; another important one. Its importance first struck me when I was reading Thomas Traherne, one of my favorite seventeenth century poets and mystics. "Certainly Adam and Eve in Paradise had not more sweete and curious apprehensions of the world than I when I was a child," he wrote. Everything was new and delightful for him. The rosy glow of sunrise had in it the flaming glory of creation. The stars at night were a living, heavenly dance. He listened to the grass growing, smelled the west wind, tasted the rain, touched the grains of sand on the shore. All his senses, his mind, his heart, were alive and in touch with *being*. "So that," Traherne adds sadly, "without much ado I was corrupted, and made to learn the dirty devices of this world, which now I *unlearn*, and become, as it were, a little child again, that I may enter into the Kingdom of God."

A lot of my adult life has been spent in trying to overcome this corruption, in unlearning the dirty devices of this world, which would dull our imaginations, cut away our creativity. So it is only with the conscious unselfconsciousness of a child that I can think about theories of aesthetics, of art, particularly as these touch upon my questions about life and love and God.

. . .

I was still at the age of unselfconscious spontaneity when I started to write. At the age of five I wrote a story, which my mother saved for a long time, about a little "grul," my five-year-old spelling for girl.

I wrote stories because I was a solitary, only child in New York City, with no easily available library where I could get books. So when I had read all the stories in my bookcase, the only way for me to get more stories to read was to write them.

And I knew, as a child, that it was through story that I was able to make some small sense of the confusions and complications of life. The sound of coughing from my father's gas-burned lungs was a constant reminder of war and its terror. At school I read a book about the Belgian babies impaled on bayonets like small, slaughtered animals. I saw pictures of villages ravaged by the Bôches. The thought that there could ever be another war was a source of deep fear. I would implore my parents, "There won't be another war, will there?" My parents never lied to me. They tried to prepare me for this century of war, not to frighten me.

But I was frightened, and I tried to heal my fear with stories, stories which gave me courage, stories which affirmed that ultimately love is stronger than hate. If love is stronger than hate, then war is not all there is. I wrote, and I illustrated my stories. At bedtime, my mother told me more stories. And so story helped me to learn to live. Story was in no way an evasion of life, but a way of living life creatively instead of fearfully.

It was a shock when one day in school one of the teachers accused me of "telling a story." She was not complimenting me on my fertile imagination. She was making the deadly accusation that I was telling a lie.

If I learned anything from that teacher, it was that lie and story are incompatible. If it holds no truth, then it cannot truly be story. And so I knew that it was in story that I found flashes of that truth which makes us free.

. . .

And yet we are still being taught that fairy tales and myths are to be discarded as soon as we are old enough to understand "reality." I had a disturbed and angry letter from a young mother who told me that a friend of hers, with young children, gave them only instructive books; she wasn't going to allow their minds to be polluted with fairy tales. They were going to be taught the "real" world.

This attitude is a victory for the powers of this world. Another friend of mine, a fine story-teller, remarked to me, "Jesus was not a theologian. He was God who told stories."

Yes. God who told stories.

St. Matthew says, "And he spake many things to them in parables . . . and without a parable spake he not to them."

When the powers of this world denigrate and deny the value of story, life loses much of its meaning; and for many people in the world today, life *has* lost its meaning, one reason why every other hospital bed is for someone with a mental, not a physical illness.

Clyde Kilby writes, "Meaninglessness inhibits fullness of life and is therefore equivalent to illness. Meaning makes a great many things endurable—perhaps everything . . . .it is not that 'God' is a myth, but that myth is the revelation of a divine life in man. It is not we who invent myth; rather, it speaks to us as a Word of God."

The well-intentioned mothers who don't want their children polluted by fairy tales would not only deny them their childhood, with its high creativity, but they would have them conform to the secular world, with its dirty devices. The world of fairy tale, fantasy, myth, is inimical to the secular world and in total opposition to it, for it is interested not in limited laboratory proofs, but in truth.

When I was a child, reading Hans Christian Andersen's tales, reading about Joseph and his coat of many colors and his infuriating bragging about his dreams, reading *The Selfish Giant* and *The Book of Jonah*, these diverse stories spoke to me in the same language, and I knew, intuitively, that they belonged to the same world. For the world of the Bible, both the Old and the New Testaments, is the world of Story, story which may be able to speak to us as a Word of God.

The artist who is a Christian, like any other Christian, is required to be *in* this world, but not *of* it. We are to be in this world as healers, as listeners, and as servants.

In art we are once again able to do all the things we have forgotten: we are able to walk on water; we speak to the angels who call us; we move, unfettered, among the stars.

We write, we make music, we draw pictures, because we are listening for meaning, feeling for healing. And during the writing of the story, or the painting, or the composing or singing or playing, we are returned to that open creativity which was ours when we were children. We cannot be mature artists if we have lost the ability to believe which we had as children. An artist at work is in a condition of complete and total faith.

. . .

I am grateful that I started writing at a very early age, before I realized what a daring thing it is to do, to set down words on paper, to attempt to tell a story, create characters. We have to be braver than we think we can be, because God is constantly calling us to be more than we are, to see through plastic sham to living, breathing reality, and to break down our defenses of self-protection in order to be free to receive and give love.

With God, even a rich man can enter the narrow gate to heaven. Earthbound as we are, even we can walk on water.

. . .

We will not have the courage or the ability to unlearn the dirty devices of which Traherne warns us, or to keep our child's creativity, unless we are willing to be truly "grown-up." Creativity opens us to revelation, and when our high creativity is lowered to two percent, so is our capacity to see angels, to walk on water, to talk with unicorns. In the act of creativity, the artist lets go the self-control

91

which he normally clings to, and is open to riding the wind. Something almost always happens to startle us during the act of creating, but not unless we let go our adult intellectual control and become as open as little children. This does not mean to set aside or discard the intellect, but to understand that it is not to become a dictator, for when it does, we are closed off from revelation.

. . .

As I read and reread the Gospels, the startling event of the Transfiguration is one of the highlights. You'd think that in the church year we would celebrate it with as much excitement and joy as we do Christmas and Easter. We give it lip service when we talk about "mountain-top-experiences," but mostly we ignore it, and my guess is that this is because we are afraid.

We are afraid of the Transfiguration for much the same reason that people are afraid that theatre is a "lie," that a story isn't "true," that art is somehow immoral, carnal, and not spiritual.

. . .

For the past several generations we've forgotten what the psychologists call our "archaic understanding," a willingness to know things in their deepest, most mythic sense. We're all born with archaic understanding, and I'd guess that the loss of it goes directly along with the loss of ourselves as creators.

But unless we are creators, we are not fully alive.

. . .

What do I mean by creators? Not only artists, whose acts of creation are the obvious ones of working with paint or clay or words. Creativity is a way of living life, no matter what our vocation, or how we earn our living. Creativity is not limited to the arts, or having some kind of important career. Several women have written to me to complain about *A Swiftly Tilting Planet*. They feel that I should not have allowed Meg Murry to give up a career by marrying Calvin, having children, and quietly helping her husband with his work behind the scenes. But if women are to be free to choose to pursue a career as well as marriage, they must also be free to choose the making of a home and the nurture of a family as their vocation; that was Meg's choice, and a free one, and it was as creative a choice as if she had gone on to get a Ph.D. in quantum mechanics. Our freedom to be creators is far less limited than some people would think.

. . .

Freedom is a terrible gift, and the theory behind all dictatorships is that "the people" do not want freedom. They want bread and circuses. They want workman's compensation and fringe benefits and TV. Give up your free will, give up your freedom to make choices, listen to the expert, and you will have three cars in your garage, steak on the table, and you will no longer have to suffer the agony of choice.

Choice is an essential ingredient of fiction and drama. A protagonist must not simply be acted upon; he must act, by making a choice, a decision to do this rather than that. A series of mistaken choices throughout the centuries has brought us to a restricted way of life in which we have less freedom than we are meant to have, and so we have a sense of powerlessness and frustration which comes from our inability to change the many terrible things happening on our planet.

. . .

"What if . . ."—the basis of all story. The small child asks all the what ifs. All of life is story, story unravelling and revealing meaning. Despite our inability to control circumstances, we are given the gift of being free to respond to them in our own way, creatively or destructively. As far as we know, even the higher animals (with the exception, perhaps, of the dolphin) do not have this consciousness, not necessarily selfconsciousness, but consciousness of having a part in the story.

And the story involves what seems to the closed mind to be impossible—another reason for disbelieving it. But, as Christians, we may choose to live by the most glorious impossibles. Or not to live, which is why in the churches, by and large, the impossibles —the Annunciation and the Transfiguration and walkings on water and raisings from the dead—are ignored or glossed over.

I see my young friends groping back toward a less restricted view of time and space, though sometimes in frighteningly faddish ways. Contemplation is sought through drugs, which can never produce it. Seances and trips in the astral body are on the increase, and the church condemns and draws back. But if we do not offer a groping generation the real thing, they will look for it elsewhere, or, they will fall, as George Tyrrell observed, for the garbage of any superstition.

It is not easy for me to be a Christian, to believe twenty-four hours a day all that I want to believe. I stray, and then my stories pull me back if I listen to them carefully. I have often been asked if my Christianity affects my stories, and surely it is the other way around; my stories affect my Christianity, restore me, shake me by the scruff of the neck, and pull this straying sinner into an awed faith.

~

When I start working on a book, which is usually several years and several books before I start to *write* it, I am somewhat like a French peasant cook. There are several pots on the back of the stove, and as I go by during the day's work, I drop a carrot in one, an onion in another, a chunk of meat in another. When it comes time to prepare the meal, I take the pot which is most nearly full and bring it to the front of the stove.

So it is with writing. There are several pots on those back burners. An idea for a scene goes into one, a character into another, a description of a tree in the fog into another. When it comes time to write, I bring forward the pot which has the most in it. The dropping in of ideas is sometimes quite conscious; sometimes it happens without my realizing it. I look, and something has been added which is just what I need, but I don't remember when it was added.

When it is time to start work, I look at everything in the pot, sort, arrange, think about character and story line. Most of this part of the work is done consciously, but then there comes a moment of unselfconsciousness, of letting go and serving the work.

.   .   .

To be alive is to be vulnerable. To be born is to start the journey toward death. If taxes have not always been inevitable, death has. What, then, does life mean? No more than "Out, brief candle"?

The artist struggles towards meaning. Mahler was terrified of death and worked out his fear in music. I had a letter from a college student at Harvard saying, "I am afraid of non-being." That same day, a friend with whom I was having lunch said, "I cannot bear the thought of annihilation."

Art is an affirmation of life, a rebuttal of death.

And here we blunder into paradox again, for during the creation of any form of art, art which affirms the value and the holiness of life, the artist must die.

To serve a work of art, great or small, is to die, to die to self. If the artist is to be able to listen to the work, he must get out of the way; or, more correctly, since getting out of the way is not a do-it-yourself activity, he must be willing to be got out of the way, to be killed to self (as Juan Carlos Ortiz sees the mythic killing by baptism) in order to become the servant of the work.

To serve a work of art is almost identical with adoring the Master of the Universe in contemplative prayer. In contemplative prayer the saint (who knows himself to be a sinner, for none of us is whole, healed, and holy twenty-four hours a day) turns inward in what is called "the prayer of the heart," not to find self, but to lose self in order to be found.

We have been afraid of this kind of prayer, we of the twentieth century Judeo-Christian tradition. It is not talked about in many temples or churches. And so those intuitively seeking it have been forced to look for it elsewhere.

Why have we been afraid of it? Because it is death, and no matter how loudly we protest, we are afraid of death.

. . .

The great artists, dying to self in their work, collaborate with their work, know it, and are known by it as Adam knew Eve, and so share in the mighty act of Creation.

That is our Calling, the Calling of all of us, but perhaps it is simplest for the artist (at work, at prayer) to understand, for nothing is created without this terrible entering into death. It takes great faith, faith in the work if not conscious faith in God, for dying is fearful. But without this death, nothing is born. And if we die willingly, no matter how frightened we may be, we will be found, and born anew into life, and life more abundant.

. . .

When Jesus called Peter to come to him across the water, Peter, for one brief, glorious moment, remembered how, and strode with ease across the lake. This is how we are meant to be, and then we forget, and we sink. But if we cry out for help (as Peter did) we will be pulled out of the water; we won't drown. And if we listen, we will hear; and if we look, we will see.

. . .

But only if I die first, only if I am willing to die. I am mortal, flawed, trapped in my own skin, my own barely-used brain. I do not understand this death, but I am learning to trust it. Only through this death can come the glory of the resurrection; only through this death can come birth.

And I cannot do it myself. It is not easy to think of any kind of death as a gift, but it is prefigured for us in the mighty acts of Creation and Incarnation, in Crucifixion and Resurrection.

Crosswicks
June, 1980

James Parks Morton

The Very Reverend James Parks Morton, B.A., S.T.B., M.A., is
Dean of The Cathedral Church of St. John the Divine in New York
City. Dean Morton has been instrumental in helping to establish
the Cathedral as an important center of religion, culture, and
creativity, hosting events that have attracted some of the world's
most respected spiritual leaders, peacemakers, artists, environ-
mentalists, and political activists. He is also an acting Board
Member of numerous social, spiritual, and artistic associations
and, in 1975, *Time Magazine* counted him among the Fifty Young
World Leaders to watch. In 1985, the American Institute of Architects honored his work in undertaking the rebuilding the Cathedral
with an Award of Merit.

97

I met Jim Morton in 1979 in Snowmass, Colorado, at an advisory meeting of the Windstar Foundation. Good fortune allowed us to be neighbors for that weekend and, staying up late one night, we began a conversation about the role of ritual, priestliness, and spirituality in our culture, a discussion which we have continued over the years. In January of 1983 I did some consulting for one of the Cathedral's programs. Jim took me to his favorite Greek restaurant (one of many restaurants in New York City where he seems to know every chef and waiter). Afterwards, happily full, we sat up late into the night recording the following interview.

*   *   *

What is your vision of what the Cathedral can become, and how do the arts relate to that vision?

The vision is first to reestablish in the vocabulary of Americans what the term "cathedral" represents. My supposition here is that "cathedral" is a very opaque word, and it has no currency for most Americans. When asked "What is a cathedral?" they'll think of having seen Notre Dame de Paris or Chartres or Westminster Abbey or something like that. They will think a cathedral is purely an historical monument of some past time that is beautiful and that has pleasant memories but no impinging effect upon life as they lead it now. This is made even worse by the fact that cathedrals —like royalty, and nobility, and concepts of that sort—represent the medieval, authoritarian Europe that Americans left behind and came to America to get away from.

A cathedral is just the reverse of that. A cathedral is urban and represents all of life. It's artistic, political, economic, social, sociological—all of these dimensions. In medieval times the cathedral was always on the market place and was indeed a holy place in the city, in the sense of being a sort of summation of all that was in the city. It was built by the tanners' guilds, and the truckers, and the goldsmiths, and the actors, and the stonemasons—all of the people who made life work in an area—making the cathedral the most perfect and complete and overflowing expression of that common life that everyone shared.

Of course there were bad times in which people felt they had to get away from the authoritarianism and oppression that became associated with the cathedral. But nonetheless, the term "cathedral" is a

European reality that has had no root in the American psyche. Here we are in America in an age when, at our deepest level, Americans of all different stripes, and persuasions, and backgrounds are striving for living images of their connectedness with everything else, which is precisely what a cathedral represented in the twelfth or thirteenth century.

What I am trying to do at Saint John the Divine is to use this extraordinary architectural, geographic, aesthetic, and urban reality to fill that function. We are physically building a cathedral, stone by stone, but we are also iconically, and artistically, and sociologically building a cathedral, trying to make it a place about which everybody living in New York can say, "That is *my* place because it is a holy place. It is New York's holy place, and I am in New York and, therefore, it is my place."

Let us think for a moment of the things that would militate against that today: people would say, "Well, I'm Jewish," or "I'm Buddhist," or "I'm Pentacostal," or "I'm Lutheran," or "I'm Roman Catholic," or "I'm Black," or "I'm White," or "I'm Oriental," or "I'm this," or "I'm that." People have tended to form their primary identity in terms of what they are in *contrast* to what other people are. That is certainly what a cathedral did not do; a cathedral was the symbol of what unites all.

Medieval society was not in any sense monochromatic; it was very differentiated in terms of social classes and roles and was very structured. Nonetheless, the cathedral was something that bound everybody together. Here in America, with the patchwork quilt of nationalities, and religions, and ethnicities, people once again are searching for a symbol—yet more than just a symbol—something in which they can participate that is bigger than all of them and that transcends the differences. A cathedral is a ready-made possibility for people to come into communion. Differences are not washed away or eroded, but are in fact transcended. By definition, communion exists only between differences; there can be no communion of identicals. It is two different realities coming into unity. So a cathedral as a center of communion, or as a place for the communion of differences, is what we are trying to build.

Another way of thinking about a cathedral refers to the skill and quality of work and of expression that people had at other times in history, modes of behavior that became stereotyped or ritualized through the practice of craftsmanship. These behaviors— social behaviors, or aesthetic, or architectural, or painterly, or sculptural—were developed through discipline. For example, meat is cut in a certain way without thinking about how to pick up the knife or fork. Or setting the table in a certain way, or buttoning a shirt, becomes an almost unconscious activity once the motor skills or standards are learned. In earlier periods of history these automatic behaviors extended to virtually every form of human interaction and were visible in the artifacts that bound people together. The objects that surrounded life—clothing, food, decoration, buildings, or furniture—were crafted in certain, given ways, and the manner of performing any craft had to be learned in such a way as to develop unselfconscious artisans rather than selfconscious artists.

This can be seen in terms of the manners—in their most extreme form called "chivalry"—that govern human interaction. There are certain ways things must be done and certain ways not to do them. But they have to be learned; they don't come with mothers' milk. They are learned and practiced, and we are scolded if they aren't done correctly. There is nothing "moral" about these manners. There is nothing "good" or "bad" about a green light or a red light. We could stop at green lights and go at red lights; it doesn't matter. It is an arbitrary decision that is made about social interaction. It is exactly the same as putting the right hand out to shake hands; we could just as well put our left hand out, and in certain countries that is done. Neither is "good" or "bad." It *is* "right" or "wrong," however; it *is* "correct" or "incorrect." These are not moral but aesthetic decisions.

It is on these decisions that the fabric, the texture of a whole civilization is built. Quality, and value, and meaning are derived from this layering of ways of doing things. Obviously, these things can become charged with "good" and "bad" meanings as opposed to "right" and "wrong" meanings. If this charging with meaning becomes really oppressive and totalitarian for large numbers of people, inevitably there will be revolution. And, as with most revolutions, the baby gets thrown out with the bath water.

That is somewhat the situation that we find ourselves in now. The sixties are rather an extreme example, but people often would say, "Don't tell me how to respond to people. I'm not going to shake hands if I don't like a person." To me it is the absolute breakdown of civilization when people "interiorize" and say they are not going to behave unless they can make personal value judgments. Civility, in its etymology, refers to the way one behaves in a city (civitas—urban living), and urban living does not mean refusing to step out of the way of a person based on personal judgment about that person. A child must give his seat to an older person even if that older person is someone the child dislikes.

These purely structural things in social convention can only be learned as a result of what I would call "the crafting of human interaction." It is an art form ultimately, not casual but very defined. It is this way and not that way. But it's what builds up a neighborhood, or a family, or a city. These are the rituals of living. Craft in art—a dance, a pot, a building, a book, a poem, a song—requires the same process of learning, and practice, and discipline, and correction. It's either "right" or it's "wrong," and if it is not "right," it must be done ten times until it *is* right. It's the kind of discipline that one has to use in practicing the piano or practicing penmanship. One might say, "I'm expressing my art in my handwriting." And the teacher could say, "But I can't read that; it's illegible." These days the student might retort, "Well, I don't care if you can't read it; it's me!" Handwriting was not illegible at the turn of the century, and I don't think people felt tyrannized just because they had to write legibly.

It is the same with someone who chops stone in our cathedral stoneyard; the master builder won't allow it to be done incorrectly. There is a way in which one's personality and that which is uniquely one's own signature will come out in that stone, but it comes out through having a mastery that would appear at first to be almost an obliteration of one's uniqueness. The stone must first be cut absolutely correctly and then, on top of that, one's personality and uniqueness is very obvious. Or, in a class of thirty kids, each writing "cat" on the board, those who can't spell "c-a-t," flunk. Once the letters are distinguishable, they can make all kinds of flourishes, and asymmetries, and nuances.

You mentioned the stoneyard. Are there other areas where the arts and aesthetics are anchoring themselves in the life of the cathedral?

The cathedral is built of the same stuff that virtually every other building is made of; they are all made of the same stone. But, in a cathedral, that stone is more elegantly placed, carved, and ornamented, and the scale is greater. Now, in America, this fundamental craft of cutting stone has practically vanished. You can say, "Well, so

C. Harrison Conroy

Finished facade of St. John the Divine. Several other sections of the world's largest cathedral currently undergoing new efforts for completion.

Robert Rodriguez

The exacting craft of stonecutting has been revitalized under the Cathedral's apprenticeship program.

102

Omega Liturgical Dance Company, artists-in-residence at the Cathedral, performing during the St. Francis of Assissi Day mass, October 6, 1985.

Beverly Hale

Beverly Hale

Procession of animals led by the Paul Winter Consort during the St. Francis Day celebration.

103

what? We have other kinds of building materials." But stone is about as primordial a building element as there is. Stone is that which we stand on, and its symbolic value is very significant. Before energy became a problem, we built out of glass. We went through a kind of fool's paradise thinking that energy was free. So we are looking again at those materials that retain heat in the winter or cool in the summer, and stone is the top building material on that score.

Another consideration is the new-found reverence for the work of generations before us. Not long ago we were confident that what we were doing was so much better than what had gone before that we could wipe the slate clean; that was our way of restoring our cities. We now look back and see that as naiveté, and hubris, and stupidity, thinking that we could just wipe away something in order to create instantly whatever we wanted. I remember U Thant saying, "We can accomplish essentially anything we want to; the only problem we have is to decide what we want to do." I thought, "My God! What a wonderful thing!" I now look back on that, scratching my head, and realize that it's daydreaming! It takes me *years* to do what I think I can do in two days. I am newly mindful of the weight of the past. So much of me is past; I carry it around. It's not bad; it's just a fact. It's who I am, what our cities are, what our lives are. Tomorrow is not simply bright and golden; tomorrow is, to a large extent, yesterday. But it is not necessarily bad that there is this kind of inertia.

We are also newly mindful of conservation. A great deal of our lives is taken up with the care of our bodies. We call it "preventive health," and everybody knows it's a good thing. Our bodies are something we have inherited, and they are going to be around for a while; so we damn well better keep them in good shape. It is exactly that sort of mentality that we ought to bring to our body politic, and our cities, and architecture. I can't just throw my body out the window and expect a new one; nor can I just throw my city out the window and expect a new one. I've got to massage that city, and paint it, and wash it, and clean it, and exercise it. If my body is made of flesh and blood, I've got to have people around who can read flesh and blood; I've got to have doctors. Similarly, if we are going to keep our cities together, we've got to have artists to be their doctors.

A cathedral keeps the fundamental artisans of the body politic at their top form because the cathedral has the best stone cutters, the best glass people, the best dancers, singers, actors, scientists, biologists, politicians. All of them consecrate their work at the highest level. A cathedral has got to see that those folks are around and are working together. The artists that the cathedral must maintain are the artists that are needed to keep everybody's lives in good shape and consecrated. A cathedral creates common art. "Common" doesn't mean "vulgar," but "public." Common art, like communion, is for everybody. It's what binds us together. So here we have artists who can bind everyone together, working at the hubs of cities—the centers where all the spokes come together. This is common art in its most noble, most consecrated form.

Twenty years from now, how will some of the seeds that you are planting here have developed?

I see the cathedral ringed with restaurants, theaters, and shops—all places of human interchange. I can see a really marvelous market, right in front of the cathedral, that is full of stuff that is handmade and full of people who are selling, and talking, and coming into communion with each other by way of their artifacts. These artifacts might be songs, dramas, poetry, quiches, pastries, goulashes, wines, cheeses, printed fabrics, printed books, crafted pots, or shaped furniture—the things that create health. Markets are wonderful clinics where people care for each other. There would be as many people selling things as buying things. Everyone would be sitting down, drinking tea or coffee and chatting. There would be lots and lots of little places, unlike the supermarket which is based on the idea that there are nine-hundred people pushing along little carts and only ten people working. I think there ought to be a hundred people buying and a hundred people selling. If everything is "untouched by human hands" and canned, we are essentially moving toward the notion of the human being as a discarnate spirit. And that which makes the world is the Spirit that is in these beautiful bodies that smell, and feel, and have textures, and waddle around, and caress one another, and can appreciate sunsets, and mud, and dogs, and things.

There has been a kind of Platonic attitude that is fundamentally embarrassed about the body: the closer to perfection you get, the further away from the body you get. The Christian faith is the resurrection of the hairy body, not just the immortality of the pure soul. The Communion, the Eucharist, the Mass, are central to Christian living precisely because they are the continual process of incarnation, of the Spirit filling and transforming flesh, matter, stuff—making it perfect. There is a tendency in all kinds of theologies to be "spiritual" at the expense of the flesh. In the West it is most typical in neo-Platonism, in which the body is essentially despised, a prison from which pure Spirit must be rescued. In some Eastern religions too, the body is beaten, and despised, and mortified, and sort of left out in the cold for the sake of pure Spirit.

But that is really not Christian, and it is very fundamentally not Jewish. The whole Hebraic tradition is the resurrection of the flesh, which is the resurrection of the earth. The earth is not something you can just get rid of. God created the earth, and it is good, and we are all part of this earth. The Christian resurrection is a resurrection of the earth, of the flesh, and of the body. The Eucharist is the eternal resurrection of bread and wine which, again, is manufactured stuff. I mean, it has human sweat in it! Kneaded bread is not just pure wheat. And the biblical images of the Kingdom of God, of heaven, are dinners—banquets with lots of wine and food! They are marriage banquets. Do you know what wedding feasts are? They're parties! The point is that they're social events and are not just some puritanical notion of disembodied spirits in meditation until the end of time.

Our artistry is in the way we bake the bread, the way we make the wine. That's an artistic endeavor, a manufactured thing, a thing that we make. What makes us artists is *what* we do and *how* we do. The artist is required in heaven. That side of us, the creative side, is what makes us most human. It's that humanness, that artistry within us, whereby we don't just take what is given, but we goose it up a bit, we make it more beautiful, more communicative. Animals aren't artists; they eat what is thrown to them. What makes us human is that we knead, and bake, and cut, and arrange what is given to us. And then we have a party! You see, it's the Communion—that we are making it for each other; that's the difference. We make it beautiful, and fun to eat, and fun to look at. The more human we become, the more artistic we become. The artist is the perfected human. God makes us artists, meaning that He makes us in the image of Himself who makes stuff, makes it beautiful, makes it serviceable, makes it fun. That's what we're meant to do.

You have said in discussions we've had in the past that artists are like prophets. What do you mean by that?

Prophecy is that irrevocable commitment to saying the truth and to living out that truth no matter how it may be received. Prophets do not live in vacuums; they say things that are always contiguous, always in context and in relationship to things that are happening. The artist also does not live in a vacuum and is always in context. The artist is driven to work, to compose or to sculpt what the Truth is, what the Light is showing it to be. That may be contrary to the more popular, accepted ways of society, but artists, like prophets, must live out a vision and enflesh that vision in the matter of their mediums. These visions of life are Spirit-given, conveyed by the Spirit. The Spirit drives artists to craft things in certain ways, to craft words in certain patterns, prophetic utterances, or prophetic poems, or prophetic pots, or prophetic whatever. Prophecy and artistic creation are very closely intertwined.

I had a discussion with a rabbi not long ago who viewed art as a kind of whore. Art would sleep with anyone and didn't really care. He used the example of art in the service of Hitler as well as art in the service of Churchill. A great orchestra could play for Hitler or for Churchill, in the service of totalitarianism or of liberation and freedom. He said that art was essentially amoral and, therefore, must always be judged by the Light. The Light is never neutral; the Light is Truth. There is truth and there is falsehood; art can serve either very beautifully.

You have artists in residence here at the cathedral. Is there a criterion by which you invite artists into the cathedral's life, such as working with Spirit in a prophetic fashion as you just described?

Those artists here in residence are here precisely because they are caught up in the larger spiritual/social/evangelical task of their art. In other words, they are not just creating art for the sake of art. It's very much art for God's sake, art for people's sake, art for the sake of the world's good.

Today the "art world" is essentially something that creates markets. It is Fifty-Seventh Street, or auction houses, or rather well-off people who are interested in art. I mean, art in this sense is a luxury, something more and more people want just as they want fancier cars, or swimming pools, or houses. It's a kind of social business. In our mercantile civilization, art is more a kind of badge of wealth and of success than what we've been talking about—art in the way one does things, the way one lives, the way one sees, the way one crafts one's life.

I see all life as art. I'm so fascinated by creation that I'm looking for patterns, and meanings, and avenues of identification in virtually everything around me. And I'm finding that the artists who are most helpful to me are those who give me conceptual tools with which I can make identifications. I am as happy looking at seashells on a beach as I am looking at the Parthenon. And what's fun for me is seeing the patterns of the volutes on the shells and seeing those same patterns repeated in the flutings of the columns and volutes of an Ionic capitol. What turns me on is tracing the patterns in a feather, and the skeleton of a fish, and in a leaf, and then in the pattern of Cezanne's trees. I go into paroxysms of joy when I line up those things! That to me is a kind of mystical experience of identity.

To me, an artist is a person who is able to give me the keys that unlock the identity behind aspects of creation and show me that they are, in fact, related. Our task now is to make it possible for people to experience unity with one another, unity with all creation. That is the religious task of our age, and the artist is our indispensable guide and teacher in the accomplishing of this task. For me, the artist and the priest are very close indeed.

Inquiries regarding the Cathedral of St. John the Divine may be addressed to: The Cathedral, 1047 Amsetrdam Avenue, New York, NY 10025.

Paul Winter

Paul Winter is the founding father and guiding spirit of the style
which has come to be known as New Age music, a style that blends
ethnic, folk, symphonic, and environmental influences. In 1961,
the Paul Winter Consort (then called the Paul Winter Sextet) won
the Intercollegiate Jazz Festival, which led to a recording contract
with Columbia Records. In 1962, the group received an invitation
from the Kennedys to play at the White House and became the first
jazz group ever to play there. Since 1980, Paul Winter has been
artist-in-residence at the Cathedral of St. John the Divine in New
York City where he composed one of his most ambitious and
popular works, the ecological and ecumenical *Missa Gaia/Earth
Mass*. Paul has his own recording label, *Living Music*, which has
released six records: *Callings, Missa Gaia/Earth Mass,
Sun Singer* (named Jazz Album of the year in 1983 by the National
Association of Independent Record Distributors), *Icarus, Concert
for the Earth*, and most recently, *Canyon*, recorded on location in
the Grand Canyon and at the Cathedral. He is currently working on
a multi-album series called *A Song of Russia*, based on the indige-
nous music and natural wonders of the Soviet Union.

109

*I first became aware of Paul Winter's music when an enthusias-
tic friend gave our family a gift of the Consort's LP* Common
Ground. *That music, a blend of rhythms from many cultures
interwoven with the songs of wolves, eagles, and whales, became
a constant backdrop to our family life and evoked from our
daughter, who was eleven months old at the time, a most beautiful dance which she repeated only three times, each time to the
Consort's music. I attended the* Earth Mass/Missa Gaia *performance at Saint John the Divine on Pentecost Sunday in June of
1984. On the following day, this interview took place in the barn at
Paul's farm in Connecticut.*

*　　　*　　　*

*Over dinner, you talked about the magic that happens when a
group of individuals work together. I would like to re-capture that
discussion.*

We were talking about the awakening of Spirit, a kind of aliveness
that we feel within and among ourselves that happens in a shared
celebration. "Wonder" is perhaps a better word to use, in that it
won't confuse people into thinking we're in the magic business.
Music has a special ability to awaken wonder in people, perhaps
more quickly than anything except nature. Take a group of people to
the edge of the Grand Canyon, or show them a puppy, and they get it
immediately. They join in a common sense of wonder. This common
capacity for wonder is what encourages me about the possibilities of
the human species, because what we are capable of in that state is
an expression of wholeness, an experience of our own wholeness
that may even surprise us.

An example of this happened yesterday and concerned two percus-
sionists who joined us in the *Earth Mass* performance. One of them
was a fellow who plays a didjeridoo (a large end-blown musical pipe
of the Australian aborigines) and had never heard our *Earth Mass*
or been in any of our celebrations. We invited him to play during
some transitional interludes, and he ended up playing percussion
with us in some of the last numbers. He instinctively knew what to
do. An African percussionist, Kimati Dinizulu, also had never heard
the *Missa Gaia* before. With very little coaching, he knew what to do
too. There's an inherent wisdom we have that comes out in a shared
situation like that, without instruction, without verbal direction

from anybody. It could be that it goes back to almost a tribal way of knowing that we had as very early humans. I love situations that call upon that.

What happens to you as an individual? Does the individual get lost in the group? Can you describe that process?

I don't know how much can be verbalized. I've heard there are three brains: the reptilian, which is the ancient survival brain; the mammalian, which is the ancient emotional brain; and the neo-cortex, which is the specifically human brain. The three of them often operate in competition with one another, or in conflict. But when they cooperate, we become phenomonally aware, conscious, and loving beings. It could be that certain activities link the three brains: jogging, for example, perhaps music-making, maybe love-making, maybe volleyball. For me, playing the *Earth Mass*, or any good concert, does it every time.

We've done the *Mass* about twenty times now. Things that you do again and again tend to be taken for granted. You're not as electrified as you were the first time. But at a certain point, the flower begins to open up for me. Almost always, at a certain point during the *Mass*, I feel the tears welling up in me. That's a rare thing for me. I don't get tearful very often. From that moment on, I'm all connected, and I think, "Of course! This is it. We're all part of this, and we are all very loving beings." And then that fades away—that epiphany, or cathar-sis, or whatever it is. It's a very precious thing. If we had it all the time, we'd take it for granted. But having it come back again and again and again really shifts something in us. We know that there is this place of sacredness, of connectedness. That's the essence of what it means for me. We know that's where we ought to be. Each time we get lost in the forest of our computer-thoughts, and problem-solving, and resisting life, and being judgmental, there's a little night-light in the back of our brains which reminds us of that place. Music gets me back to it, and so does being in nature.

Obviously, you were successful, through the Earth Mass, *in evok-ing that in the congregation. What goes into creating a work of art that has the ability to evoke such a deep response?*

"Work of art" is a loaded phrase. When you talk to somebody who has supposedly made a "work of art," you may be putting them on a

111

pedestal. I know that when I put somebody up there, I feel distanced from them in a way that is unfair to them and to me. I feel best when I resonate with people. The writer, Scott Nearing, would say to me, "Well, grab a hoe and help me turn over this compost pile while we talk about it," rather than approach me like some ninety-five-year-old sage who's got some special goodies. Everyone has some special goodies.

The *Earth Mass* is a case-in-point. I haven't thought of it as a "work of art," though it may qualify as that, and that's okay. But it's more important to me to see it as a living organism, because it is continually growing. Gordon Bok, the folk-singer from Maine, says, "A song is a vessel you fill with your living." The *Earth Mass* is a vessel that we fill with our living. Each time we play it there are some new pieces in it, new improvisations, or new instrumentalists, or new ways of doing things. The *Mass* was and is a collective creation, the product of many people. My role, besides playing saxophone in the *Mass*, has been as the envisioner, the catalyst, the weaver, and the entrepreneur.

Can you say a little about those four roles?

We became artists-in-residence at the Cathedral of Saint John the Divine in the fall of 1980, and early in 1981 the Dean of the Cathedral, Jim Morton, asked us to create some twentieth-century music for the mass. This was an astounding proposal for me, since I had never even been to a mass, and knew very little about the forms of liturgical music. I recall sitting in the Cathedral for my first mass, late in January, 1981. We had given concerts in the Cathedral, but only on Saturday evenings, and I hadn't really been "in church" for twenty years. I had stayed as far away as I could. Amory and Hunter Lovins were giving the address that morning, talking about solar energy and the earth's resources, and things very pertinent to my life and my heart. I realized that perhaps things that I cared about could be relevant there in the Cathedral. You see, I had never put that together before. I always felt that whatever I cared about was far away from church, and that the church had little interest in any of my concerns.

The vision for *Earth Mass* came while I was listening to Hunter and Amory. I imagined hearing joyous, rhythmic, and physical music during the Sunday ritual, and voices of wolves and whales resounding in the extraordinary acoustic space of this Cathedral. I wanted the Cathedral to resonate with a sense of wonder for the whole earth. Afterwards, I asked the Dean if we could call our mass *Earth Mass*, and include the voices of animals as well as our Afro-Brazilian rhythms. He said, "Absolutely," and I was quite surprised. I would have thought there'd be very strict guidelines for a high mass. It was astounding to me that every idea I came up with during the next six months was acceptable. Our only requirement was to include the basic mass texts; beyond that we could do almost anything. So I began listening to recordings of some fifty masses. I didn't necessarily want to adapt music that had been done before; I just wanted to see how it had been treated by different composers. The mass is an enormously flexible form, as it has been for eight-hundred years.

Then, acting as a catalyst, I brought the first ideas to the Consort for a free-form brain-storming session. I brought in my overall vision, and shared whatever I knew about the context for the project: the form of the mass; that it would be performed in the Cathedral, with choir and pipe organ; that it absolutely had to have the four mass texts—Kyrie, Sanctus, Benedictus, and Agnus Dei. But beyond that we were free to include any music under the sun. I explained my vision that our mass would celebrate the entire earth as a sacred space and would include the voices of our animal friends/musicians. We began sharing ideas, finding clues here and there—words from our own diverse religious backgrounds, Indian chants, whale melodies—and we tried various seed-themes and rhythms on our instruments, improvising them either into life or oblivion.

Then my job as weaver began. We always tape our rehearsals, and I listened to the musical ideas on those tapes and found things that really worked from those improvisations. Some of the best ideas came when we weren't even working on the thing at hand, and somebody would start playing a chant they remembered, or what-ever. I transcribed them, developed them, and took them back to the others. We did that again, and again, and again; there were about twenty-five sessions in all, utilizing our earlier experiences in group work. During the summer of 1977, for example, I had gathered some twenty musician friends here at the farm to make the album *Common Ground*. I invited all my favorite musicians, from all idioms—jazz, folk, symphonic, African—to come here. We disco-vered then that amazing things could happen in the interactions among diverse musicians if we live together in nature, sleeping and eating outdoors, making music every day, and telling each other about our lives. The synergy and the spontaneous creativity that happens when people work together are often much more valuable than the things we think of alone.

So, the *Mass* grew in a cumulative way, similar to the way Stravinsky composed. He'd be working on a piece, and on the wall he'd pin up all kinds of articles from newspapers and magazines that he had read, things he was interested in—conflicts in the world, or discoveries in science, or whatever—and each day new ideas would come, and the music would grow.

That spring of '81, when we had about half the *Earth Mass* done, I told Susan Osborn I wanted to find a song that everyone could sing— the congregation and the chorus—a hymn with a lyric that would be non-evangelical, since I didn't want any evangelism in the *Mass*. I suddenly remembered that she had sung a hymn to me when we were sitting in the car outside a laundromat in Rapid City, South Dakota, six years earlier, when the Consort was on tour on the West Coast. She had sung *For the Beauty of the Earth*, and I loved it. Susan right away remembered the hymn; it just came right back. So two minutes after posing the question of where to find a universal melody, and one that celebrates nature, we had it.

In the broadest sense of my aesthetic experience, this song rang a bell, because I remembered the feeling of being in church so many Sunday mornings as a kid, and the feeling of people singing together. When I hear a band marching down the street now, it really gets to me, because that's what we did back in Altoona where I grew up. It's people doing something together, sharing it. And that's a very moving thing to me. We have all too little of that in our society now.

The story of making the *Earth Mass* inspires me because of all the different threads that came together from different individuals. For example, Kim Oler came to see me regarding business. We were looking for someone to work with our Living Music Foundation. He was with the Yale University Development Office as a graduate student and fundraiser. I didn't know he was a musician. We had dinner, and as he was leaving, I gave him a tape of the *Earth Mass*, which we had already performed once by that time. Three weeks later, Kim gave me a cassette of a new tune he had written at the piano; it had no lyrics, but I liked the melody and the harmonic motion. So I took the tape with me on tour, to play for the other musicians. It happened that I had planned a meeting in San

Francisco with Rusty Schweickart, the former astronaut, to learn more about his experience of seeing the earth from space. And Rusty quoted to me the words from Robert Heinlein's science fiction character, Rhysling, the blind balladeer of the spaceways:

We pray for one more landing
On the globe that gave us birth.
May we rest our eyes
On the fleecy skies
And the cool green hills of Earth.

It occurred to me to see if lyrics, based on these words, could be put to Kim Oler's new tune; so I called Kim and recited the poem. When we returned to New York a few days later, he presented us with the song, *The Blue Green Hills of Earth*, which we recorded as part of the *Earth Mass* the next week. So this song was a gift—from Kim, Rusty, and Heinlein - and my role was as weaver.

Can you talk about the fourth role that you mentioned, the entrepreneur?

The entrepreneur takes responsibility for getting something out into the world, all that's necessary to actualize a dream or a vision. It includes a lot of coordination, networking, fundraising, financial risk-taking, and time. And it's the bane of probably every artist's life, right? It's the thing that we don't want to have to deal with. We just want to do our thing. There are people who do their thing early, with grace, and get on a greased track and have other people stoking the engine for them. I have always looked at them with amazement and, sometimes, no little bit of envy. Early public success hasn't been my fortune; or conversely, I could say that I've had the good fortune not to have it be that easy. The best possibility is that it might ground the work, deepen the work, might prevent you from thinking that you did a "work of art," or that you're an "artist," whatever that is. It definitely keeps you clear that you're just a person.

Some time ago you mentioned your evolution from a jazz musician to someone who now creates and performs "sacred" music. Can you talk a little about that? What were the turning points?

There's no difference to me between my current music and that of twenty years ago, in its essence. If jazz, in its broadest sense, reflects the musical expression of experiment and adventure that has taken

115

place in America, then it embraces everything I've ever done. There were times when I was aligned with a more narrow sense of jazz, a kind of nightclub gymnastics. But still within me was the same yearning to reach out to many people, to resonate with many people. I just didn't know how to express it then.

The context I was immersed in during my early twenties was be-bop jazz, and that aesthetic excluded many people. We thought we were kind of "over there" from people who might go to church or to symphonies, or people who listen to folk music. When we're young, one of the ways that we sometimes choose to affirm our strength and our confidence is to champion our own thing and damn the others. I hated folk music. I couldn't stand those singers and their corny songs. Three or four years later, Peter, Paul, and Mary were among my best friends, and Paul was producing our first Consort albums. As I grew, I realized that there were many possibilities for soulful expression.

Going to Brazil was a turning point for me, and hearing the humpback whales was a milestone. But mostly it's been a gradual evolution or expansion, or perhaps a gradual return to the wholeness that was there in the beginning. As a little kid I didn't have all those barriers set up in my mind. There were just people, because kids are very accepting. Then we go through our education, our adolescence, and our struggle to find place and identity and relationship in the world. But as we grow, we slough off those identifications and become more accepting.

In fact, your music now is really a hybrid in terms of form. It's not folk song; it's not religious song; it's not jazz. Yet it can be any of those things at a given time.

Yes, the labels become less important to us, and to me that's the best confidence that I can see growing among us. We would not have that confidence, though, had we not had an audience that has grown along with us, that has accepted us as we are. We used to think that we had to do a very special thing with tremendous expertise in order to have an audience. What we were doing was placing our own judging minds out there in those seats, and censoring ourselves with our own little private supreme court, when really, human beings and audiences most want you to be yourselves. They don't have nearly the expectations that you have of yourself. The more we have allowed ourselves to be corny, vulnerable, human, the better it's gotten.

116

When you dream ahead, do you sense new frontiers for your work?

Yes. There's a universal music out there that could be the most powerful shaping force in the cultural life of the human species. I get more and more intimations of this each year. Sometimes we touch on it. It's a music that involves the participation of everybody present; the chorus howls that we do with audiences are the beginnings of that. But I think that shared music-making is an almost undiscovered mode in our society, certainly undiscovered in relation to the predominance of print and talk in modern cultures. Print perpetuates a fragmented experience of life, whereas sound—in music as opposed to words—is experienced with the whole of being. It almost doesn't matter what message is transmitted; it's the shifting of people into being whole and therefore less judgmental, less excluding of one another, and more accepting of life.

Some music unites people, but not necessarily into love. So there is a shadow to that process as well. Do you ever concern yourself with that?

I've thought about that, and I appreciate what you're saying. There is a worry that music can be used in that way, once people learn how powerful it is.

It's the music people goose-step to, marching in rows.

All the nourishing things in life have that double potential. Water is the great nourisher; yet we can drown in it. Fire keeps us warm; yet it can burn us.

I could say honestly that for thirty years of my life now, since 1954, I've had to endure a culture that was dominated increasingly by what I regard as infantile music, music that is reflective of the machine-dominated existence of life in cities. As cities grew larger, machines took over more and more, media became more powerful, and the people became more sheep-like, therefore more gullible. Music had to pound louder and louder every year to attract their attention. But these are my people in these cities, the people of my times. And I want to send them back a gentler song.

117

In my own work as a musician, I want to make my music gentle enough so that it can trigger, yet not replace, the inner music of the listener.

Yes, and I can't envision a turn-around of the city madness. As long as media is in control, it will prey upon the lowest common denominator; it will prey upon the gullible. The more flashy something is, the more attractive it's going to be to the gullible, and they won't notice the subtler things. Much of nature is quite subtle. Not many people get to be in nature enough to shift this need for highly-spiced foods, and flashy music, and laser shows, and naked bodies, and bizarre horror movies.

Your practice, then, is to be nourished by nature, to listen to the subtleties and somehow find a way to communicate that through your music?

Yes, that's part of it. Another part, though, is what we do as a group—that synergy—and bringing that group into nature. I had seen what happened to a group of people when we had them out-doors in Baja, California for a week together. Doesn't matter if there are whales there, or gurus, or whatever. Just outdoors. We're amazing beings, and we cut ourselves off from our potentialities by staying inside square rooms all the time. Thoreau said: "Most of our troubles are house-bred."

What else do you do to prepare yourself? What are the elements that you feel are absolutely essential for you as a human being and as a musician?

Time with myself is real important. That's the only way I can get the wheels to spin slow enough to see what the patterns are. It's very easy to gather the stimuli, very easy to get the inspiration and all the clues. So the challenge for me is to let it all digest and reveal itself. I don't think I could do much of my work in New York City if I lived there all the time. What New York invokes is the entrepreneur in me. When I'm in New York and wake up to all that noise going on, I feel I ought to be on the phone talking to people and stirring up projects. I am very much affected by the environment that I'm in. I marvel at people, like my friend Gary Snyder, who feel that they can work anywhere. He could probably write poetry on Forty-Second Street. I can't think there of anything but escape.

It's interesting. Most of the things that I can think of in answering this question deal with slowing down the mind. This amazing tool we've been blessed with is also our biggest problem; the thing that solves problems also makes the problems.

Are you working on any new projects or albums?

Yes. We've been working on an album about the Grand Canyon that's almost done. We're going to Russia to work on an album series called *Song of Russia* about the beauty of nature and wildlife in the Soviet Union. It'll be a whole album, like *Earth Mass*, about the beauty of their land and their culture, and the way they love it, the way their culture relates to nature. The point is that those people love the Earth as we do, and nature may be our common ground for peace.

There are about thirty other albums on my wish-list, several of which are in progress. We have recorded an album with Gary Snyder, improvising to his poetry, that will be called *Turtle Island*, after his book. We'll go to Africa, after the *Song of Russia* series is launched, to begin work on music celebrating the great mammals of that continent, who are desperately close to extinction and need help.

There is no shortage of ideas. For much of the last twenty years I have had no outlets for the albums I've dreamed of. Now, thanks to the growth of our audience, some luck, and a lot of "entrepreneuring," we have our own label, *Living Music Records*, and we can now go to work on the wish-list. I'm deeply grateful for this, and that I live in these times, and in this remarkable and blessed garden called "America."

For further information about Paul Winter's work contact: Living Music, Box 72, Litchfield, CT 06759.

Betty Freeman

Dane Rudhyar

Dane Rudhyar worked for over sixty years to transform the assumptions and patterns of thinking which structure the way of life in our Western culture. His accomplishments in the fields of music, philosophy, astrology, psychology, painting, and literature earned for him the accolade of twentieth-century "Renaissance Man." Yet he preferred the term "Seed Man," for he claimed that we are not living in a classical age in which culture "flowers," but in a period in which the end of one culture-cycle interpenetrates the beginning of the next and comes to "seed" in and through a relatively few promethean pioneers. Through his vital interest in oriental and occidental philosophies, he has formulated a dynamic and compelling "philosphy of wholeness" which is outlined in numerous articles and thirty published books which include: *The Planetarization of Consciousness; Beyond Individualism; Culture, Crisis, and Creativity; Fire out Of The Stone; The Magic of Tone and the Art of Music; The Astrology of Transformation* and, most recently, *The Rhythm of Wholeness*.

121

*When the idea for LIGHTWORKS came to me, Rudhyar was the
first person I thought to include.* Culture, Crisis, and Creativity, *in
which he expressed his ideas concerning creativity and the role of
the individual in the transformation of culture, was a book that
illuminated key issues for me. I continue to be inspired by his
perceptions. The following article, written in 1984 for this book,
sums up many of Rudhyar's central themes and explores the
opportunity for transformation that our time offers. Just before this
manuscript was sent to print, on September 13, 1985, we heard
that Rudhyar had died at the age of ninety.*

*   *   *

THE ULTIMATE CHOICE

Vulgarization or Transcendence

The basic factor in any attempt to interpret and evaluate the
character of creative activity, either in the arts or in the fields of
philosophy, psychology, or social organization, is the state of the
culture within which the creative activity takes place at a particular
time. A truly creative process is an answer to the collective evolutionary need of a society, which is determined by the phase of development reached by the culture to which the creative person
belongs. The need is answered *through* rather than *by* the creative
person.

To highly individualistic human beings who assume that they are
a "law unto themselves" and independent of their environment,
their culture, social class, family tradition, and even their peer-
group, the idea that creative activity is an answer to a collective need
rather than a personal emotional eagerness for "self-expression" is
likely to appear irrelevant. In our modern Western world, particularly in the United States, creativity is now presented as an essential
function of personhood: every person can be, and indeed should be,
"creative."

In my opinion however, no human being can be called a "person" if
he or she does not actively participate in a sociocultural relation to
other persons. A human being, living since birth on an isolated
island, without any contact with other human beings, cannot be
considered a "person." He or she would be only a living organism

122

belonging to the species Homo sapiens; his or her "personhood" would be only an innate potentiality. Necessary to the development of personhood are the examples provided by a family and social environment, the use of a definite system of communication, a language, the development of a mind given a specific form by this language, and the basic symbols, assumptions, and ways of life of a culture, however primitive they may be. The possibility for a human being to develop a particular type of personhood occurs within certain limits set by the state of his or her culture. Society is what it is long before a new human being is born into it.

Similarly, the principles according to which all living organisms operate are inherent in the planetary system of organization which we call the biosphere. At one level of planetary evolution, "life" operates as an ever-changing balance of anabolic and catabolic biological forces. At the next level, "culture" emerges from human cooperation and the organization of social relationships. A culture is the frame of reference for containing and nourishing the dualistic interplay of mind and feelings within the psyches of the human entities participating in its relations and activities. Human togetherness within the organized field of a culture generates psychism, somewhat as the combined operation of billions of cells within the organized field of a "body" produces the phenomena associated with "life."

A culture develops when a sufficient number of psychically destructured, confused, and hopeless persons, whose forebearers belonged to disintegrating cultures or subcultures, are stirred by the vibrant experience of the power of a new revelation of human purpose and destiny. The experience at first is individual, but it becomes contagious when people are compelled to interact and cooperate under the pressure of crucial circumstances. A group reaction is generated. It may lead to collective martyrdom or to a relative isolation (geographic or psychic) permitting the formation of new forms of social organization and communication, new myths and signs of recognition.

This unfolding process of the genesis and the embryonic development of a culture should be interpreted, I believe, as operating at the level of collective psychism, not as a series of individual actions called "creative." The culture forms itself through the individual human units interacting within a more or less well-defined field of experience. On the one hand, as part of the evolution of humanity, an archetypal structure—that is, a new principle of organization and relatedness—seeks to become actualized at a particular level of human consciousness and concrete group behavior. On the other, interacting human persons respond to the possibilities inherent in the archetype and in the historical/social circumstances. Moreover, the human beings' response is also conditioned by their inherited genetic and social backgrounds and by their personal experiences. The resulting culture develops out of the interplay of these several sets of possibilities—archetypal, social, and personal.

Creation is the art of the possible in relation to the evolution of mankind on the planet Earth. The fundamental reality is the planet as a whole, not only as a mass of physical matter, but as a cosmic being which has a mind and soul of planetary scope and which evolves, albeit at a pace which seems immensely slow to a human mentality limited by a relatively brief span of existence as a biological organism. Nevertheless, the planet evolves. And humanity evolves, gradually fulfilling its specific function within the vast planetary field through a series of cultures constituting wholes of collective activities and psychic energies. Each culture, at each phase of development, has specific needs and seeks to satisfy them through persons who are born at certain times and under conditions which make them particularly sensitive to these needs. The culture creates through them. The fundamental factor in creative activity is therefore the relationship between the would-be "creative" individual and his or her culture. The creative activity itself expresses this relation, even if this fact is obscured by the personal reactions of the human being as a self-seeking "expression."

∼

If the foregoing is considered a valid interpretation of the social as well as personal phenomena covered by the term "creative activity," the conclusion is that any relevant and truly significant evaluation of contemporary art (as well as all modes of sociocultural acivity, from international politics to family behavior, education, and marriage) must begin by considering the stage of development which our now world-dominating Western culture has reached. What is possible for any potentially creative person depends on what that phase is.

The most basic of the intuitive realizations which have structured my approach to life as a potentially creative person came to me in

Paris during my seventeenth year, in the fall of 1911. I realized that all processes of life had a cyclic, thus rhythmic, nature and that what, in Europe, was called civilization referred to a series of cultures, each of which was born, matured, and decayed, as do all living organisms. Moreover, I realized that the European culture in which I had been born, and which had formed my mind and my basic responses to psychological and social living, had reached a phase of disintegration which could be symbolized as the autumnal period of an entire cycle of existence.

The beginning of the first world war (1914) seemed to me an obvious justification of my intuition: the fall season and its storms had come, and everything I have experienced during the seventy-two years since then has confirmed my interpretation. Humanity, led by Euro-American society and its cultural paradigms, is in an autumnal period of disintegration; everything is falling; a process of vulgarization is evident everywhere. Societies whose collective psyches and social activities had once been structured very differently from one another are eagerly and undiscriminatingly accepting the products of this vulgarization. The amazing success of Western technology feverishly accelerates this vulgarization, reducing every qualitative value to quantity and material aggregates.

If a culture is an organic whole which grows, matures, and decays, and if the truly creative person acts at all times in answer to the need of the components of this whole, it follows that creativity during the fall season of a culture must be basically different from creativity during the spring. The fresh, spontaneous, and form-building activity of life during the vernal months is replaced after the fall equinox by different processes: leaves fall and decay into relatively undifferentiated humus, and the seeds that have matured within the fruit during summer drop to the ground. Yet some seeds, though surrounded by decay, have the power to retain their structural integrity and generic identity. They contain the power of life renewal which the entire species has focused within them, the transformative and creative power of planetary evolution.

Today, persons having emerged from a state of unconscious subservience to and mental identification with their disintegrating cultures can be found on all continents; they may legitimately be called "seed persons." Yet the process of symbolic germination—and therefore a "rebirth" of culture—may still be far away. Eager idealists, dreaming of an "American Renaissance," may have to wait for a sociocultural winter to pass. The mass vibration of today's monstrous and chaotic cities reveals the relentless operation of the principle of cultural entropy—the trend which, in spite of external differences of race, class, and wealth, reduces every activity and mode of consciousness to statistically tabulated meaninglessness. This is chaos, not the vibrant beginning of a new cycle.

What can a seed do in such a psychic environment? As it falls away from the rotting fruit, it loses its integrity and starts to decay if it has not experienced deep within the core of its being a new "belongingness," not to the particular plant that mothered its growth, but to the entire vegetable species; not to a particular culture, but to humanity; not to a particular land, but to the planet as a living, feeling, thinking, and spirit-releasing whole, a system of planetary organization which itself is part of a more inclusive cosmic whole.

This experience of belonging to a different, vastly more inclusive field of consciousness and essential activity is the first and most basic foundation which a truly individualized person needs. The inertial power of biological and sociocultural "roots" no longer operates in a fully matured seed; a new power is needed, or at least the realization that sooner or later such a power will become available. This power can be experienced as the communion of all free seed-individuals. In a still more inclusive and unified sense, it can be experienced as the "soul" of the planetary whole. Persons may experience this soul as "God," unreservedly dedicating themselves to His presumed will as formulated by a sacred revelation and interpreted by a church, or even as truth directly and personally "heard" in transcendent silences or prayers. But free individuals experience it as an impersonal and more-than-individual archetypal reality. The fact that a seed belongs implicitly and totally to its species is the only guarantee of its survival, because this fact alone relates the seed-being to a source of power, to a new rhythm of being.

~

The seed analogy which I have been using must not, however, be taken too literally. No cell in a plant has to choose between being part of a leaf compelled eventually to fall and decay, or part of a seed containing the future possibility of rebirth through germination. Biological processes have often been used for their symbolism: mystics refer to their sublime experiences as "union with the Beloved," or liken them to the intoxication of "wine," and the Bible symbolizes the earliest occult Brotherhoods of our present humanity as Noah's "vineyards." Nevertheless, such symbolizations tend to obscure the central factor defining the essential character and function of the human state, the natural evolutionary transition between two basic levels of being: that of "life" and that of a higher, far more inclusive state of being, to which I have given the gnostic name "Pleroma." The vast tidal flow of planetary evolution passes from the one to the other through a transitional process which takes the form of the human species, Homo sapiens.

The history of mankind—past, present, and future—is simply the series of phases necessary for such a transition. It is, in this broad, evolutionary sense, a long rite of passage in which the energies and instinctual compulsions of "life" are transmuted into the powers and imperatives of the quasi-divine state of Pleroma-being. Culture and the condition of personhood are the means for that transmutation and each social, religious, and political organization constitutes one small scene in that great ritual. At the threshold of the Pleroma level of being, conscious individuals of all origins emerge from bondage to their cultures and are integrated into a spiritual state of conscious unanimity and singleness of purpose. Yet the Pleroma also includes functional differences; as in the biological realm, the Pleroma is a structured and organized system of activity, a "living" state of being, not merely an ideal.

The rite of passage from "life" to Pleroma may be divided into three main periods or "Acts." During the first, societies, their cultures, and the type of mind and personhood these make possible, are almost entirely dominated by the rhythms of life energies. During the second, mind seeks to free itself from the power of biological imperatives, and the persons of a culture strive to become independent, autonomous, and self-determined. They individualize and, as they do, the culture's psychism loses its binding power. Left unchecked, centrifugal impulses lead separative egos to struggle for power and to worship the Moloch Profit in the guise of liberty. This Act is now being performed in today's monstrous cities.

A third Act can be expected once the inevitable sociocultural reaction to the second has exhausted its potentially catastrophic possibilities. It is in this third Act that the concrete reality, meaning, and power of the Pleroma state will become increasingly evident to human beings. An ever greater number of individualized persons will feel an inner urge to experience the all-human rite of passage in themselves, in their own individual being. While this all-human rite has a planetary super-individual character, it must be experienced by every individual aspiring to join the Pleroma communion of transhuman beings. It must be experienced individually, consciously, and willfully, because the prerequisite of the Pleroma state is the full development of individual selfhood, autonomy, and personal responsibility.

Homo sapiens emerged out of the matrix of "life" (the animal kingdom of the biosphere) in order to make possible the development of these prerequisites. At the present stage of planetary evolution, the most valid and most essential goal of any fully aware individual should be to assist and participate in this passage from "life" to Pleroma, allowing the power of planetary evolution to focus itself through his or her personhood. Any activity so focused is transpersonal, but its source is metapersonal, beyond personal desire or ambition. It is a truly creative activity.

～

A "creative minority" (to use the phrase of historian Arnold Toynbee) emerges from a culture when the process of vulgarization accelerates past the point at which its momentum can be controlled or stopped. Yet even the presence of seed persons is no assurance of vernal rebirth. Swept into the decay of wet autumnal leaves, they, too, could disintegrate. The individualism of the seedhood state does not guarantee the integrity of the seed during winter. Symbolically speaking, the seed can be sustained only by a vivid, indestructible determination to remain an agent through which the species can reproduce or mutate. At the human level, the power within the inner being of seed persons is not the power of "life," but the power of a constantly and willfully sustained total consecration to the Pleroma.

In order to perform successfully the rite of passage leading to the Pleroma state, the performer must *be* that consecration. No longer a mere person, he or she becomes the Act itself, a transition state of intense motion and transformation. His or her whole being is like a bell summoning all human beings who have ears to take a ritualistic step toward the next stage in human and planetary evolution. Through that step the future is created. This is creativity in the deepest sense of the term. It is the only truly significant creativity today, though the popular, anarchistic psychology exhorts all human beings to strive after personal growth.

This does not mean, however, that what today are called the creative arts have no valid place in modern society. The basic issue is the purpose the arts are currently made to serve and the quality of the energies they put to use. The term prophetic art may be applied to whatever announces a process of cultural disintegration as well as of rebirth. Should individuals aspire to the contribution of new forms and the invention of new procedures which only accelerate the process of entropy toward psychocultural humus? Indeed, is this the way to alleviate the boredom and restlessness of individuals who are dissatisfied with the rigidity of obsolete ancestral patterns which are rooted in a distant Mediterranean past? Self-styled creative artists attuned to the intellectually self-indulgent mentality of an aroused youth can choose to hide their own and their public's emptiness or can instead deliberately use the products of a dying culture—out of which they are emerging as participants in the great rite of passage of humanity—as the most convenient and acceptable means to incite wherever possible a contagious urge for transcendence.

To present an ideal of personal transformation along ethical and cultural lines or to describe a social utopia is one thing; to induce a contagious will to become transformed by actually and persistently following a path whose meaning can only be gradually revealed by the act itself of "walking" on it is something else. It is far easier to persist in the belief that an absolute chasm exists between God (or hierarchies of divine beings) and human beings who may only reflect the ineffable state of being of the Deity. Even the now fashionable belief that a "perennial philosophy" underlies all the religious and philosophical systems of the last three to five millenia fails, I believe, to present a truly basic picture of the planetary destiny of Man, because the "perennial philosophy" does not positively state, in an evolutionary sense, what is actually and concretely possible for human beings. A very difficult choice presents itself to the individual who is irreducibly convinced that human individuals can become divine, if they choose now to deliberately and knowingly participate in the rite of passage that leads to the Pleroma.

Seen from the broadest point of view, an activity bringing to focus through culture any phase of the development of human consciousness serves a purpose. The activity of creative artists can be such a focusing process, but its meaning and its relevance to the fundamental function of humanity can be fully understood only in terms of the stage reached by the culture within which it takes place. There are cultural periods during which the character of creative activity is entirely determined by the culture. Today, when the general popular trend toward vulgarization and psychic disintegration is almost overwhelming, the process of individualization also introduces the possibility—only the possibility—of a fundamental choice. The creative artist may choose the type of energy which he or she will bring to a concrete focus in his or her work. This, not merely the technical skill of the artist as craftsman, is today more than ever the important issue.

For further information about Rudhyar's work contact: Rudhyar Institute for Transpersonal Activity, 1639 Eighth Avenue, San Francisco, CA 94122-3717.

John Todd is President of Ocean Arks International, a research and communication organization developing advanced ecological projects. OAI publishes *The Annals of Earth Stewardship* and is currently developing an "Ocean Ark," or hope ship, for the transport of biological materials to ecologically damaged regions of the world. With Nancy Jack Todd and others, he founded the New Alchemy Institute which was instrumental in developing the principles of the bioshelter, an integrated solar and wind-powered food and shelter system. He and Nancy are co-authors of a number of books including: *Bioshelters, Ocean Arks, City Farming: Ecology as the Basis for Design; Reinhabiting Cities and Towns: Designing for Sustainability*; and *Tomorrow is Our Permanent Address: The Search for an Ecological Science of Design as Embodied in the Bioshelter*. John serves as President of The Company of Stewards, Inc., a design firm which has developed and successfully tested a self-contained growing system, the Desert Farming Module, and as Executive V.P. of Forbes & Company, Inc., an international marine resource company. He is also Founder and Senior V.P. for Research of The Four Elements Corporation, a firm which develops advanced energy and shelter technologies.

*Though John's reputation is primarily that of an innovative
scientist, I have always seen him as a visionary who works to
make real the poetic images of large sail ships carrying seedlings
to ecologically devastated areas of the worlds, of cities and homes
that could integrate food production and wilderness, and of
international cooperation. He visited in March of 1985, and we
met for this interview.*

*   *   *

*You have been involved, for years now, with innovative works in
the technological, biological, and architectural arenas, and the
sum total of your images and aspirations is the creation of a
fascinating world. What experiences in your background led you
to so many avenues of exploration?*

A modern scientist, who has an active or not very active imagination, basically tries, methodically and carefully, to find out more and
more about narrower and narrower aspects of the universe, so that
the penultimate perfect scientist is a person who knows an infinite
amount about very, very little. I don't work in that world at all,
though I'm trained in it. I pull together threads from disparate
places to create patterns and possibilities that are latent in the
world and haven't been revealed. To find the origins of all that. . . .

My mother was an amateur painter and art buyer and worked
with many art galleries as we traveled throughout the country.
Things like architectural lines, and forms, and aesthetic relationships in the rural Canadian countryside were the subjects of a great
deal of conversation. When we would come upon a form that was
interesting or perfect, it would be much remarked on. My father was
a businessman with a deep, passionate concern for the wilderness
and for farming. He was also deeply interested in the design of
sailing ships and yachts of all kinds. In fact, he designed some
himself. We had endless conversations concerning the relationship
between form and function, which were never academically resolved, but which were argued about at great length. There was a
kind of invisible schooling going on in all this.

We lived at the edge of the water on one end of Lake Ontario. My
bedroom was no more than a hundred and fifty feet from the water.
To the east was a large marsh; to the north was a mixture of wooded
ravine and farmland which wound its way up through orchards and

clay hills to the Niagara escarpment that ringed the area. On the opposite side of the lake, only three miles away, was a steel company, Stelco of Canada, which became responsible for the ultimate demise of this biologically rich area. I was actually present for the death of most of the fish species. The farms and streams and ravines became asphalt and concrete. Over a period of about the first ten years of my life, everything that was wild was stolen from me.

But, in fact, this experience had some very interesting ramifications for me. I studied agriculture and biology and then went on to study parasitology and tropical medicine. I did a Master's thesis on the parasitic diseases of fish in a lake in Quebec and went to work with an environmental consulting firm. Our job was basically to look up the rumps of Canadian industry from Vancouver to New Brunswick. I went back to the steel company across the lake to convince the manager of the need for careful environmental monitering. Meanwhile, the slag was building up and moving across the lake several hundred feet each year. I went into his office, which looked across the three miles to where my home used to be, and listened to him say, "Pollute! Man, you want me to be concerned with that? Pollution is a sign of our economic vigor. I won't be happy until all we've got is a channel for the ships in here." It's not hard to imagine the radicalization that was going on in me at that particular moment and the need to be outside of the industrial world for a while.

When did you start creating alternative ecological designs?

I have a natural tendency to link things, so I finished a Doctorate combining three fields: animal behavior, fisheries, and oceanography. I was considered to be an upwardly mobile and successful young scientist. I went to San Diego to be a professor, to teach ecology. At that time I was very involved in the environmental movement, analyzing the ills of modern society, its chemical industry, its weaponry, its alienation from nature. I thought that by being the Director of a prestigious center for environmental studies, I would be able to address these problems. So I was prematurely promoted to a number of elevated positions within the university in order to accomplish this.

At some point I went through a period of reflection, questioning whether one could be useful in an orthodox institute, whether one could really be a strong force for change. I came up with a "no."

There are as many protective mechanisms in academia as there are anywhere else. So a group of us, including Bill McClarney and Nancy Jack Todd, started meeting on a pile of sand in a courtyard outside my office and talking about it. One day, I came up with the concept of "the new alchemy." I didn't know anything about alchemy at that time and nothing about the Hermetic tradition.

Did the name come out of the blue?

I had found, in an issue of Arts Canada a couple of years earlier, an article about a man who etched tiny images in small stones on Vancouver Island. This man called himself a "New Alchemist." That is the only possible precurser to the name that I can find. Of course, it's logical that the term would come out of an artistic sensibility. Basically, the Hermetic tradition during the Renaissance was, in a sense, artistic. Art was the vehicle to discovering the delicate balance between the notion of the macrocosmos and the micro-cosmos.

That metaphor became very important for the science that I subsequently explored in which each piece is a tiny mirror-image of the whole. So, in making a small greenhouse filled with plants and soil and water and fish and things—what we call a bioshelter—the relationships inside are built in planetary relationship, since that's the model I have. In a way, I work as a new alchemist in the most profound sense, trying to work out of a sacred context. And that kind of thing is very hard to convey to a group of people if you have no interest in being a guru. I could have had a methodology, and we could have called it "Sacred Architecture," and I could have had a group of people trying to figure out how it was done. But I didn't want to create teachings around my method, which forced me more and more to become an artist.

So again, the image of myself as an artist was reinforced because, by being so broadly connected, I was also in a very lonely position. I have been involved in collective artistic processes, and some have been very exciting, but I expect something hot has to be happening for them to really work. Increasingly, I see the need to break down the barriers between what is practical and applied and what is aesthetic. And maybe the final push for me was being in Bali with Margaret Meade and seeing an integrated culture where those distinctions aren't made, knowing that it is humanly possible to live in a world where your breath is taken away by everything you see.

Winston Churchill once said that we create architecture, and architecture, in turn, creates us. If that is true, bioshelters would create very different human beings than traditional buildings.

I just phoned Nancy, three thousand miles away, to check the temperature because I was concerned about the fish in the pond that heats my house. Now I could automate a computer to control it, but then I would lose that caring, and that orchestration, and those direct connections. Our house is part bioshelter, with a small fishfarm and garden within. Though the house is traditional in appearance, what would normally be a shingle roof, in Cape Cod architecture, is glazed on the southern side so the sunlight permeates the whole house, and the starlight and moonlight can march across the sky for us each night. There is a deep sensibility that can be created when human forms and nature are woven together.

Parallel to the disappearance of species of animals and plants, we are also witnessing the disappearance of human traditions. You mentioned Bali, where a synthesis between the human and natural worlds, and between the aesthetic and functional, has been practiced throughout the ages. But that kind of beauty is fading, and I think we are really improverished because of it.

In some cases, even the physical basis for the artistic expression is disappearing. For example, those incredible dugout canoes, which can be seen in so many parts of the world, are carved out of single trees. But the trees are now being cut down and sold to buy outboards and gasoline. It seems there is some mystique associated with the power of the West. To those living in a place where the horizon is a horse-ride over the pass, and suddenly there are helicopters and jet aircraft and great gleaming automobiles with four wheels, all turning at the same time and going places—the gamut of what I would call overt aggressive technology—this so superior power must be overwhelming. To top that off, some of the miracles of modern medicine must seem pretty impressive to people who are used to much more subtle psychological cures involving plants and shamans and such. It's amazing how Western technology has swept through the world. But the first onslaught is over. The world is starting to change, and rather dramatically. There's been time enough to see the side effects—the crimes, the violence, the break-downs—so in no way can we go back to what was; that's impossible.

This rise of ecology in the West may be the way in which we are seeking our spiritual roots; or maybe the rise of ecological awareness is the native people's way to tame us. I can imagine ceremonies that various native peoples might conduct in which their prayers go something like this: "Make them see the drop at the end of the leaf in dawn's first light. Make them hear the sound of the birds singing at the beginning of the day. Make them learn how to smell and not kill." I wouldn't be surprised to hear that such things are going on. It's very interesting, though. I attended a conference where I shared the platform with a Native American spiritual leader who talked about the old ways. The information was important, and I could really hear it. But when he heard me talk about the biological hope ship and all, he didn't make the connection that we are co-conspirators. He saw himself as one of the first people and therefore very different from me and the audience, little realizing that the basic stuff of life, the genetic separation between us, is so infinitesimal that it takes our finest instruments to determine the differences in gene types. So the step that would allow us to work together hasn't been made, and I don't blame the Native Americans because how do they know it isn't one more trick? How do they know I am not coyote, about to do another trick?

In the very first issue of The Annals of Earth Stewardship, *I read an article in which you described your experiences of an integrated farm and its tie to the land, and to the animals, and everything else. Are there still islands of that kind of living, or are they all gone now?*

The particular farm that I described was in Java, and as far as I can tell, it was an anomaly as the result of the peculiar topography of the area. In many of the closely surrounding areas, westernization was separating the culture of fish from the culture of rice, using big machinery. Machines, as we currently know them, are separative. They could be redesigned to integrate, but with a few exceptions, they separate.

What do you hope your work will lead to?

In the very broadest sense, I hope that my work will lead to the realization by humanity that it is possible to bring back thousands of years of ecology in a period of one or two generations. We can bring back a planetary Eden. The secrets in nature are so profound that if we worked with her in an interactive way, what is now desert could be forest, what is eroded hillside could be deep meadow and treeland. I would like to see a reverence for wilderness become so important that it is not seen as something "out there," like a park, but that the whole country could be laced with threads of wilderness. Tentacles of wilderness could reach right to the center of Manhattan, and you could walk on that path all the way to the Arctic circle, or to the Gulf of Mexico, or to San Francisco. There could be a continual pathway for all creatures instead of the currently discrete and shrinking islands of wilderness. We could learn to miniaturize the production of food, so that food could be grown in small spaces, like rooftops and streets, and we could give the land back to itself.

In the cities we could have, for example, translucent silos, perhaps shaped like statues, housed with thousands of gallons of water that is exposed to sunlight in which fish would grow, like the solar aquaculture fishponds we've created. The city could also be purified by this partnership with the natural world. For example, certain shrubs and plants are known to filter out lead and some of the nitrogenous ingredients in fuels. The air is also sacred, and the wasteproducts of our activities must be removed from it. I am not one of those people who wants to destroy cities; I simply want to bring them into balance. I want to also bring more awareness to our waste processing. We now know of ways to put waste above ground in solar silos, exposing them to light and achieving purification right on the spot. This purified waste can then be recycled. Some of our modern hotels, with atriums of plants and fountains, are caricatures of what we will see in future architecture. They use nature for cosmetic purposes, which must not be confused with the idea of partnership with nature, but even in these hotels you can begin to get some sense of the possibilities.

I also think the major mistake of American cities, one we cannot do much about for a while, is that the skyscrapers have stolen too much light. They have really turned their backs on the sun. Only the people at the top can get sunlight.

You sound so matter-of-fact when you say that, in two generations, the natural world can be restored and the Earth made green again. Do others share your optimistic view?

No, not at all. We have not developed to the level where world attention can be caught. For example, I'm trying to do a restoration project on a semi-arid Greek island, and I have gotten nowhere. Currently, I've designed a technology, called a desert-farming module, which would be a key element in the restoration process. I did that, in part, to create an economy around ecological restoration. Restoration projects now are seen as repairing the damage, rather than creating something that is economically viable. So, trying to bring together the economical, the aesthetic, and the ecological is the next step. For example, no one has yet figured out how to restore the great copper mines of the Southwest; they are just vast, ugly wastelands. My idea is to link many thousands of these desert-farming modules into long chains. A desert-farming module is a cylinder which is filled with water. This cylinder can be placed on toxic ground, and because it does not directly interact with the ground, it will not be poisoned. Inside each aquatic eco-system are fish which derive their feed from the organisms within the water. The more light, the warmer the water becomes, the more efficient the system works and, within limits, the faster the fish grow.

It is ideal for the desert, then.

Yes. On the surface of each pond, to stop evaporation, is a raft. In the raft, vegetables—lettuces, tomatoes, whatever you want—are grown. This system grows vegetables and fish in quite an abundance. Each pond would bleed out a small amount of its nutrient-rich (from fishwaste) water—weeping from the tank and running down the side. At the base of the tank, on the north side, we would plant copper tolerent desert organisms. The idea here is that the economy would have as its incidental by-product the restoration of the desert. An ordinary corporation wouldn't be interested in restoration, but in the way I want to set it up, restoration is almost incidental.

How soon can the tanks be taken away?

In five years. The plants would be well enough established with enough organic matter accumulated on the surface to provide protective covering for a permanent vegetation. Then the cylinders can be moved to another spot. The whole system could be a great producer of food, and a deserted and wasted place would come back to life. The same principle could be applied in Ethiopia, for example. But until I demonstrate it in America, in the God-forsaken environment of the devastated copper mines, no one will believe it. We have theoretically proven every facet of this system; now we have to show that it works.

So increasingly, as I think of the ecological restoration of the planet, I see the larger task as global stewardship. I am angered when I walk into a toy store and most of the images of transcendence are rocketships, machines with no life in them. Space explorations and rocket ships seem to be the dominant images depicting our notions of the future. I prefer something that is imminent and Earth-tending, but as powerful as those space images. Out of that grew the idea of a great sailing ship, an ultra modern biological hope ship within which hundreds of thousands of trees and fish and beneficial organisms, compost organisms, seedling gene stock, and such would travel under conditions of proper quarantine and be allowed to begin to restore the ecologically ravished planet. More importantly, it would carry people from various cultures who would share their information and knowledge in the places to which they would be invited.

Out of this idea grew an ocean-farming module, a technology for living on the sea and farming on the sea. But all these ideas feed on each other, and they are all beautiful. They have to be, because they are up against tough competition. NASA satellites and spacecrafts provide very compelling images. Look at all the scientific magazines which carry information of future scenarios; you never see a tree in the pictures. A lifeless planet is being cast into our imaginations. I want to foster life-filled images.

One way to fertilize the imagination with these life-affirming images would be to create a movie. . . .

I would love to do that. I have not yet found a filmmaker of stature who would be interested.

What I respect so much about your work is that all that you create is positive and non-reactive.

That was a very conscious decision on my part. There are lots of clever people chronicling what is wrong, but there is almost no

John and Nancy Jack Todd reviewing sketches of their various prototypes.

curriculum at any university that deals with making things right. It is also a question of survival. I mean, if it physically hurts every time you see the destruction, then you've got to do something.

Do you think that most people are simply blocking that pain?

I have no idea. Is our world satisfying enough for most people? It is as if the spirit of the Earth is crying out, and maybe only a few people are hearing that message.

If you would be granted one wish right now, how would you use that wish?

If I were only allowed to do one thing more, I guess I would go to Greece and marshall as much as I could of the remaining organisms left from the ancient Mediterranean world, from the various backwaters and genetically stumped trees (because all the straight trees were cut for ships and such). And I'd take what remains of the gene pool there, add a bit from other similar places throughout the world, such as Chile, California, and parts of Australia, to create a base of plants and creatures. And one day, in the not too distant future, there would be water flowing again, and forests, and Pan playing his pipes. And the gods would sing.

For further information about the work of Ocean Arks International, write OAI, 10 Shanks Pond Road, Falmouth, Massachusetts 02540. For information about the activities of the New Alchemists, write The New Alchemy Institute, 237 Hatchville Road, East Falmouth, Massachusetts 02536.

José Argüelles

José Argüelles describes himself as a transformative artist, poet, art critic, and visionary historian. He was educated at the University of Chicago where he received his Doctorate in Philosophy. He has taught at several universities, amongst them Princeton, University of California at Davis, the Evergreen State College in Washington, San Francisco State University, and University of Colorado at Denver. His books include *Mandala* and *The Feminine - Spacious as the Sky*, both co-authored with Miriam Argüelles, *The Transformative Vision: Reflections on the Nature and History of Human Expression* and, most recently, *Earth Ascending: An Illustrated Treatise on the Law Governing Whole Systems*. Currently, Argüelles is involved in the formulation and coordination of various globally tranformative projects, including the Planet Art Network (PAN), the World Day Project, and the Banner of Peace.

I read José's book, The Transformative Vision, *soon after it was published in 1975, and it became a powerful influence on my own work by its emphasis on both history as a mythic cycle and the visionary role of the artist. I have visited José on several occasions, most recently in August, 1984, during which time I interviewed him for this book.*

*   *   *

What is the relevance of art in a culture such as ours? To what degree do artists need to incorporate new dimensions in their work in order to be relevant?

My first thought is that we do not have a "culture" right now as much as a condition of transition. Our culture is like a plant that looks relatively healthy, but its roots are rotting away; it is dying. But at the same time, as in the nature of all organic processes, there is another factor or force coming into being. I would describe the old order as the first force: the order that is manifest in the Soviet political structure, in the present American political structure, in the spheres of influence in which any political structure tries to maintain control, including the Third World countries that define themselves in the dynamics of the Soviet-American world. The basic fallacy of this first order is that there is a separation between man and nature, where human intelligence is seen as something greater than the natural order. This is an anthropocentric fallacy.

At the same time there is another force rising. This second force can be seen in a small percentage of the human race: certain elements of aboriginal cultures, certain groups of people associated with the peace movement and holistic "new age" movements and, to a certain degree, some avant-guarde spiritual communities. This force is not yet manifest as a coherent phenomenon and, to the people of power and leadership in the first force, it barely exists. They know it is out there, but to them the people involved are primitives, kooks, people who do yoga, and so forth.

The concept of some common spectrum of interest that is global in nature hasn't quite occurred to people in the second force, much less in the first. It is imperative that these people become conscious of their commonalities. They also must become conscious of the fact that their power lies not in contrast to the first force—because the strength of the first force can simply demolish all opposition—but in the ways that are attuned with nature. Nature is infinitely more vast, intelligent, and powerful than the ideologies of anthropocentric belief systems. People of the second force must rise above any kind of ideology and become, at the very least, transnational. That is the first step to thinking in a transpersonal way and then in a transcendental way.

You're suggesting that there is a progression from a transnational interest that leads to the transpersonal and transcendental?

Yes, and all three add up to transformation. For example, people say, "We are not getting anywhere; we are spending a trillion dollars a year on arms. Why should I support my government?" Finding other people in other parts of the world who are thinking the same thing starts to light up the way to thinking transnationally. This is already subversive for the first force.

And then there is a certain logical progression from transnational to transpersonal. There are two key issues: one is that there be some sense of development of consciousness or awareness of the earth as the ultimate concern. If we destroy the planet, then we can't even talk in terms of our survival. And along with some kind of global awareness, there must be an intensification of human-to-human levels of communication that are not based on ideologies or belief systems.

What does art have to do with this? If you think of art as some way of decorating the environment or if you think of art as prestige, it has very little to do with it. But art can be a form of enlightened behavior that is constructive, done out of compassion, not only for human beings, but for the environment and for the planet itself. We can't deal with the deteriorating world situation except through really imaginative behavior.

Having set the context, I think it would be wonderful if you would give some examples of this second-order art.

In some ways there has been no real manifestation of a second-order art yet, though we can see its embryonic form in a number of areas such as performance or ritual art, or theater which emphasizes some type of human catharsis. In order to achieve a very high order of unity between people, there has to be some kind of cathartic process.

The so-called "earth art" is another seed, an attempt to under-stand how the very elements of the environment work as artistic forces themselves. The artist here is the person who facilitates or directs these processes in such a way that communicates height-ened awareness.

In the visual arts there is a tendency toward symbolic art forms, forms that work with mandalas or with architectural structures. And some of the social forms that arise out of communities with ritual processes are discoveries about how humans bond with each other. If we go back to the aboriginal level, we see healing circles, and medicine wheels, and forms of personal or social processes that put one more immediately in contact with the deeper cosmic experience of things. There are also high-tech processes of syn-thesis.

All of these are embryonic forms; we can see the seeds of what is possible here. This kind of art is very different from the art in galleries, or professional theater, or the entertainment industry. We're talking about participatory activities that put one much more in touch with actual, natural, elemental processes and orders.

So in some ways we need to reach way back in history to pre-industrial existence, and we need to move forward as well.

This is why I speak of "bringing about the aboriginal future." I'm not talking about throwing away civilization, though a lot of what we have is really unfit. The point is that we are moving to a more aboriginal state of things. As you probably know from my previous works, *Mandala* and *The Transformative Vision* in particular, 1986-1987 has been a critical point in my examination of the historical, civilizational process. I discovered that this year, 1986-87, corresponded to a transition in the Tibetan Kala Chakra Wheel of Time which is based on sixty-year cycles. The seventeenth of these sixty-year periods begins in 1987. The ancient Mexican calendar and the related teachings of Quetzalcoatl show 1987 to be the conclusion of the ninth of nine fifty-two-year periods which began in 1519. Studies of the prophecies that have gone along with these two cycles have all led me to believe that this is going to be a very critical period.

Last summer (1983) I became involved with the World Day Com-mittee. We set our sights on the summer solstice of 1986 for World Day, which fits completely. World Day will be a synchronized, global event, operating on a much higher level of consciousness than its predecessor, Earth Day, in 1970. Earth Day brought ecology to planetary awareness. Now the situation has gone completely critical; Earth Day was an early warning, and this is "red alert."

But isn't it also a signal of opportunity?

Yes, it's a great opportunity. If everything works properly and everybody does what needs to be done, then the second force will actually become coherent, articulate, a network-of-networks. Like a bridge from history to post-history, from the decadent, barbaric situation of the present to the aboriginal future, the network-of-networks is a bridge that will be in place by World Day and the summer solstice of 1986. The first force will recognize that indeed there is a second force. We don't know to what degree the first force will have deteriorated at that point, but the engagement of the first and second forces will create synergy; a third force will be born. It will be interesting to see what the third force is all about. In my own work with the Planet Art Network, I am in the process of formulating a vision for that third force which will culminate in the creation of a genuine planet artwork.

Can you say more about this planet art project?

As you will see when you examine my new book, *Earth Ascending*, the planet art project is defined in terms of three fields: electromagnetic, gravitational, and biopsychic. The biopsychic field is the field of consciousness; the electromagnetic field includes the radiation belts and all the energy generated from them; and the gravitational field is the geomagnetic force of the planet. These fields all function in mutual resonance and actually define our experience on this planet.

There are key places, like the Grand Canyon or Mount Rainier, and also sacred sites, like Stonehenge or the Great Pyramid or Machu Picchu, that are the nodes. The planet artwork will be to identify these places and to have people begin to work with the energy there. The ley-lines—the lines drawn between the nodes —may be defined by implanting crystals at those places. We will bring in the high-tech—video, computer, and satellite systems—as well as all the synthesizer systems for sound, and light, and color performance. And so, at a number of the key places, we'll be having synchronized light and sound displays. At a synchronized moment, there will be a planet-wide program of light-sound manifestations occurring. There will be participatory medicine wheel rituals or other participatory rituals occurring at the same time. In this way, Planet Art Project synchronizes time, space, and people and creates a ritual of global proportions.

How will you include people of different traditions? For example, the Medicine Wheel might not be applicable to someone from another tradition.

On a generic level, the Medicine Wheel creates a circle; everyone knows a circle. The plan—I refer to this as the Pan-Art Network Plan - is obviously to allow for local variations and for local understanding of what works at each place to enter into the situation. Whether it's at the geomantic level of finding the ley-lines and nodes, or through the ritual healing circles, or the high-tech synchronization of light and sound, the key is the submission to the larger order of things, the planetary order, what I refer to as the process of "holonomic resonance." A lot of people are attuned to this, particularly aboriginals; it doesn't need to be explained to them. The numbers of people involved are not the point. Nor is the world knowing about it the point. The point is the synchronizing, the finding of a sufficient number of people to realize that this could happen, to be willing to make it happen, and to understand that a larger shift is occurring.

So you are looking for individuals who can serve as priests and priestesses in an act of sacrament really. And the congregation is humanity, the whole earth.

Yes. And it doesn't matter whether they know about it, or whether they want it, or whether they don't want it. What matters is that a critical number of people are willing to play the catalytic role for one day.

Early in December of last year, I was in Los Angeles, and I had a vision. It was very simple. It came to me as an "aboriginal future" news bulletin, and it described this event taking place on the dawn of August 16, 1987. It was called "The Earth Surrender Rite," in which a number of people, on behalf of the rest of humanity, surrendered to the planet and let the planet or planetary powers know that a sufficient number of people were willing to work with whatever directives or imperatives come from the hierarchical order of nature. That was how it came to me.

Harley Swiftdeer, who is a North American Indian shaman, gave a lecture on the prophecies for the years 1984, 1985, 1986, and 1987. This is what he said about 1987: "One hundred forty-four-thousand sundance enlightened teachers will totally awaken in their dream-mind bodies. They will begin to meet in their own feathered-serpent or winged-serpent wheels and become a major force of the Light to help the rest of humanity to dance their dream awake. A sundance teacher is any human being who has awakened, who has gained the dream-mind body, and who honors all paths, all teachers, and all ways. I look for the day when I can sit down with my pipe and the Buddhists with theirs. You will see me sit down with my dagger and my Sufi drum, my sword and my Shinto Way, and my pipe, my Indian way. We're going to put our soul out on the table and say, 'I love you all!' This is the sacred dance; that's what 1987 is about. That's a sundancer. You cannot say that you have the only true way, for all ways are true."

Was this in direct response to what you were planning?

No, this was independent. What I had written is right here in the *Aboriginal Future News Bulletin*: "At sunrise, August 16, 1987, the first missionaries of the Aboriginal Futures Group of the Art Army of the Planet Art Network surrendered to Planet Earth. Following the Dawnbreak New Fire-Lighting Ceremony, principle emissaries at key planetary points lay down their bodies in circular formation, heads toward the fire, feet outward, on their backs, gazing skyward. These emissaries constituted the first wave of humans to surrender control, thus allowing the terrestial hierarchy to assert harmonic command. Rendering unto the Hierarchy all ego-control, the emis-saries of the Aboriginal Futures Group chanted the New World into being. From this primal utterance, the harmonic command of hierarchy channeled through the emissaries. The New World dawned. Planetary harmonization had completed itself; planetiza-tion had just begun, and everywhere radiance gathered like clouds."

That was my statement. When I discovered Harley Swiftdeer's statement, some six months after my particular vision had come to me, it was a strong confirmation of this particular plan. I know many aboriginal leaders all over the world who are attuned to this and, as I've talked with people, it has become apparent that the information is spreading and people are synchronizing themselves with these ideas. I am asking people all over the world to observe, in small groups, moments of unconditional commitment to wholeness, to our planetary future, to love for all beings and the environment, so that as we build up this synchronization process, we strengthen the resonant field. Through such exercises we build up to this date of August 16/17, 1987.

Right now, artists whose consciousness, commitment, energy, and will are inclined in this direction have an incredible opportunity to synchronize a critical sacred level of human imagination and consciousness with cosmic coincidence. By working with cosmic coincidences, celestial and telluric forces that are interacting at these key times, we can actually make that shift. Planet Art Project is a subjective act, symbolically enacted, which works with planetary timing processes.

Have you tested these principles in your own life?

The experience of synchronicity, like coincidence—not anticipating that two things will be brought together—is to everyday human experience what the manifestation of lightning is to the whole electrical process. Just two-hundred years ago we hadn't tapped into the energy that lightning represents. Likewise, we haven't tapped into the energy that synchronicity represents. Synchronicity is the key factor in what I've been talking about. More and more, I've learned to trust and work with it. To trust in working with synchronicity is to trust in really letting go of your ego and your personal desire.

You work in resonance with the creative rhythm.

Exactly. When you start doing that, letting yourself go into it, there can be an increase in these synchronistic coincidences in very spectacular forms.

How do you reconcile this spontaneous availability to synchronicity with something that really requires planning and organizational work? It seems to me that organizations tend to squeeze out that availability and often are non-synchronistic.

Synchronicity is like a door that opens up in the right hemisphere of your brain, and then the left hemisphere, your data analyzer, says, "Oh, we can do this and this." The important point is to be completely flexible in your planning; further synchronicities are always going to alter your plan.

So organizations must understand this synchronicity, or the momentum of inertia, of expectations, will prevent synchronicity from happening. Perhaps what are needed are organisms and not organizations.

That's absolutely correct. That's why I spoke of the network-of-networks itself as a transitional phenomenon, as a bridge. Who knows? The important point is that we have to build the bridge, and we have to get across the bridge. We are going to succeed. We're not going to blow up. Actually, what the new evolutionary cycle is about is preparation for entrance into what I refer to as the Community of Galactic Intelligence.

So you believe this shift will happen relatively gracefully.

Well, I know that the shift is going to happen, that we are going to enter the next evolutionary cycle. It's not going to be without its problems. I think it would be rather foolish to think that somehow a magic wand is going to be waved, and people are going to wake up and say, "Oh, here we are in this magic land, where we always wanted to be!" It's not quite that simple.

But you are saying that, instead of kicking and screaming into a new world, we can consciously bring it forth.

As the magical members of the second force realize their bonding with all the other magical members of that force and maintain their resonance with the planetary wave that is now occurring, the flavor/aroma/aura of that activity will help magnetize and heal people who are still enmeshed in the nightmare of the first force. So we must look at the establishment of rehabilitation programs on a massive scale to help people. Economic things have to be considered. There are a lot of factors involved.

One more question. We are here in your office, and on the wall is a diploma from the University of Chicago for a Doctorate in Philosophy. How did the transition occur from Doctor of Philosophy to "wizard?" You think like a magician.

When I was in high school, in my tenth-grade English class, I wrote a report on what I wanted to be when I grew up. I wanted to be a Doctor of Philosophy. I thought that meant, literally, Doctor of the "love of wisdom." I wanted to become a doctor who could heal through the love of wisdom. I'm sure that everybody thought I was the kinkiest guy in the class. But I knew that was what I was aiming for. I realized, obviously, when I went to the University of Chicago in the 1960's, that it meant something very, very different. But I never lost my vision.

I also got a Doctorate in Art History. Both degrees were roadmarks in my attempt to understand better what I felt to be wrong in the world of art and in the world in general. I used that as a base to intensify my study of global civilization and of different cultures. Through that study and through my own spiritual practice, I arrived at the spectacle you see before you today.

For further information about José Argüelles' projects write: Planet Art Network, 262 Spruce Street, Boulder, CO 80302.

Richard Chamberlain

Richard Chamberlain is a respected film, stage, and television performer who has become one of America'a best known actors for performances in three acclaimed television mini-series: *Shogun* and *The Thornbirds*, (both of which brought him Golden Globe Awards for Best Actor,) and *Wallenberg*. His credits in film roles include *The Last Wave*, by Australian director Peter Weir; in television roles, the series, *Doctor Kildare*; and on stage, *Hamlet*, performed in England as the first actor from America to play the title role since John Barrymore in 1929. Chamberlain has his own production company, Cham Enterprises, at Burbank Studios in Los Angeles. Currently he is beginning production on a new CBS mini-series, *Dream West*, based on the novel of the same name about California pioneer John C. Fremont.

Each time I've met Richard, I have been struck by the mysterious mixture of a very private person and the public persona that I—and millions of others—have come to know from his performances in dramas which speak a humanistic and universal language. In April of 1984, I visited Richard at his home in Beverly Hills and, though we were interrupted by numerous phone calls and urgent mail deliveries, we managed to take a couple of hours for the following conversation.

*   *   *

When I was a little boy, halfway across the world in Yugoslavia, I watched Doctor Kildare *on television; the show was as popular there as it was here. That was twenty years ago. At some point you went to England to try Shakespearean acting. What made you choose to change your career?*

The basic concept of what I imagine an actor to be was formed when I was in college. I went to Pomona College here in Claremont, California, and had a wonderful director and teacher, a frail little old lady named Virginia Princess Allen. She wasn't a very good classroom teacher, but she was a superb director. In those four years at college I acted in many plays, classical and modern. I began to understand an actor as somebody who did everything, from Shakespeare to cabaret, somebody who sang, and danced, and fenced, and rode horses, and played the piano, and the whole caboodle. One week I could be some broken-down degenerate, the next week a king, and the next week an ordinary insurance salesman. That to me was the fun; that was the magic; that was the glamour and the excitement of being an actor: being many, many different people.

I loved doing the *Kildare* show, but by the end of five years I felt very constricted by it and had a tremendous urge to branch out. I was always attracted by the British stage: the sense of discipline and the way they trained and worked. I liked what I heard about the seriousness with which they approached their art and craft. Having grown up in Hollywood, I sensed that there was a different value system there, and that turned out to be true. Hollywood is a wonderful town to test your spirit in because the tide in Hollywood runs toward money and popularity, and the immense power they bring. It runs toward symbols of power, symbols of achievement. It doesn't avoid art or expertise and skill, but it doesn't appreciate them on their own.

I found, when I went to England, that nobody cared what kind of car you drove; nobody cared anything about how much money you made. They cared about how good you were. I found that most of the actors I was working with did television and film simply to make enough money to go out and do repertory in the summertime. That's where their hearts were; that's where they could do Shakespeare and all the material they really loved. Of course, there were exceptions, but I was gratified to know that being a good actor was enough. So I turned my attention to being a good actor, which has been a very arduous and long process. I always feel achieving that is just ahead.

How were you received as an American actor doing Shakespeare in England?

The British were incredibly generous. I did a lot of work with the director before we actually went into rehearsal, and we worked after rehearsal every day. It was an intense crash course in how to play Shakespeare. I found everybody I worked with very generous, though what they said in the dressing room when I wasn't there, I don't know. I think they were all kind of worried that my development seemed so very slow during the first four weeks. But I made it, and I was accepted seriously by the press. They certainly did not say that it was the greatest *Hamlet* they had ever seen, but they took me seriously in the part and said, "This is an actor to watch." That's more than I could have dreamed of. They were very, very generous to me. I got on with the British very well. I think they understood that I came as a student.

What did you learn there?

It's awfully hard to put things in categories. One learns from example more than most anything else, and the example of both acting and directorial skills was deep, and rich, and wonderful. Good British actors have a way of bringing on a whole lifetime the minute they enter a stage or appear on screen. It's less usual to see American actors do that, though some can. Often when I go to British theaters I find that even the smaller, supporting parts are played by superb, though little-known actors who can walk onstage and somehow convey the quality of the room they've just left, what they've been doing, and the general quality of their lives. That takes an incredible gift and skill. Also, the directors seem to be deeply concerned with the personal details of the characters and the exact structuring of relationships. They aren't content to rely just on words or production values as an easy way to get by.

And then you decided to come back to the United States. . . .

When I first went to England, I thought maybe I'd stay there; I loved it so much. But after about four and a half years, I got homesick. It's funny . . . a bit like being invited into a wonderful club where everyone is incredibly gracious, and generous, and warm, and couldn't be nicer in any way, or more loyal. But somehow you never quite belong; you're always a guest. That's how I felt. I wouldn't trade those years in England for anything, but it was time to come home.

You said that you feel your mastery as an artist, as an actor, still lies ahead. Can you describe what that might be, what is still ahead for you?

Yes. The pattern of my life, as I see it at the moment, has been a process of identifying and leaving behind learned behavior and replacing it with spontaneous behavior; leaving behind, little by little, preconceived ways of thinking, of behaving, of relating to people. I'm letting whoever I really am out of that strange entrapment of preconceived ideas and expectations which I apparently acquired very, very early in my life. In my work that would translate into becoming a lot more spontaneous and responsive in the moment. That doesn't mean that I no longer need technique or skill; it means that after I have put in all the work, and all the thought, and all the time into creating a character, I can let the character live, without being overly careful, or preconceived, or cautious about performance.

Can you give an example of an actor who embodies this quality?

Sam Shephard. I love watching Sam Shephard on screen. I can't believe that he also writes plays! To be so talented is amazing. He is personally present on screen. Consequently, he has the unique power of an individual who is like no other individual. That's what we don't trust in ourselves. We spend so much time either trying to be like an image we've created or like somebody else we think is better than we are. We don't trust ourselves to *be*. That's why these actors—like Sam Shephard, Debra Winger, or George C. Scott when he is at his best—are so riveting; they invest what they're doing with aspects of themselves which are totally unique.

You have spoken about how you abstract or bring to the surface an aspect of your being. What do you go through, say, to act out a king?

The process is not very intellectual, for me anyway. I don't say, "Hey, part A-five and part seven-Z, come out now!" What I do is immerse myself in the material. I read the script over and over again; I read the source material over and over again. If the project is taken from a novel, I read the novel many times and, in a half- conscious way, invite appropriate parts of myself to come forward. It's a sense of allowing the focus of my being to gravitate toward the applicable parts of myself. Then these parts feel gradually more confident, and they begin to form the character themselves. After a while, I begin to read the lines like the character; I begin to move like the character and to get ideas about clothes, and inner feelings, and intentions.

So you take on a considerably changed identity. What happens to your own identity at that moment?

My normal, everyday self stands to the side to a certain extent— hopefully more and more as time goes on—and observes, watching from some point and telling me whether or not I'm fulfilling my intentions—almost like a director. I rely on that point of observation. But I always have to find the balance so that it doesn't become intimidating either, like an authority figure saying, "Oh no, bad scene, very bad." When that happens on stage, or in front of a camera, the character, like a child, pulls back and won't come out with freedom to show himself. Then I become overly careful or overly calculated.

When you prepare for a role, how do you know that you have found that new identity and can speak as that character and not as Richard?

When the character takes on an authenticity, a feeling of life, a feeling of its own vitality. You know, an author will tell you that as he writes a novel the characters come alive in his mind and tell him what to do, how to write them. Developing a character in acting is somewhat like that. Notes ring true; sounds ring true; the way a phrase is spoken rings true, and it feels alive.

Is your personal life affected by the characters you play? What happens when you switch from one role to another? Do you, Richard, need to assert yourself in between?

I don't take my characters home with me as much as I have heard that some actors do. But a character can flavor your life, especially in the theater. In playing the same part, night after night, there is a little tint that lingers.

And developing a new character is rather painful; I find that I always have to go back to zero. The first rehearsals, the first few days of shooting, I'm at zero again. It's as if I've never acted before. The first rehearsal, the first read-through, I haven't the faintest idea who I am, what to do, how to say things. I haven't got a clue. It's a feeling of nakedness, of intense vulnerability. And then, with luck, the character begins to take form. It's a fascinating and rather mysterious process, exciting and painful all at once.

I remember reading an interview with Peter Sellers in which he said that amidst the many identities that he took on as an actor, his own identity was lost in the shuffle. Do you ever experience anything similar?

No. In the past I haven't experienced it because I needed to cling so tightly to a preestablished idea of who I was. Now that I am really beginning to enjoy who I authentically am, I find that my real self, in all its complexity, is gaining considerable solidity. Not solidity as in lack of movement, but as dependability available to me and to my friends.

Is that a new thing in your life?

Very new. It's a slow exchange of old images with new. Krishnamurti talks about "the new" all the time. The mind, according to his definition, is always concerned with memory and cannot encompass "the new." Words can never capture "the new," because that moment is just ahead of words. That's where Life is; that's where excitement is; that's where acting is, and that is where I want my acting to reside more and more.

You have now been acting for some twenty-four years. Do you act because it fulfills you personally, or do you see your acting as a service to other people?

I have been served by actors, dancers, and singers. They have reminded me of the immense vitality, beauty, variety, pain, and creativity of being human. And I would like to be of service and in some way illuminate for others the treasures of life. When I am operating at full steam, and my work takes me by surprise because it's coming directly from whatever my creative source is, I find my conscious mind asking, "Wow, where did that come from?!" When that process is happening, I am aware of being connected with the whole of the play, the whole of the character, the whole of what's going on in a way that the conscious mind could never conceive. And in that sense, certainly, the source of creativity is mysterious.

Is that a common occurence in your work?

The sense of being in that poised position, where energy and creativity are flowing with complete freedom, is unusual to me. It's rather rare. That state is easier for me to find in the theater because playing the same material night after night brings a familiarity which invites experimentation and the relaxing of technical control. There's a speed in filmmaking that works against transcending control. There's a great deal of pressure to do it right, right away, and anybody with any skill can do it right, right away. I can do it right, right away, because my mind's quick, and I can figure out what's required, and I know how to do it, within the bounds of the preconceived, for want of a better phrase. But to really "let her rip," to really let the creative force rip right through, requires a tolerance for the unknown, a tolerance for making a time-consuming mistake.

To what degree do the text and the role assist in that flow?

I find that, to the degree the role is conceived well, it has a genuine life; it has genuine vitality, and it aids my whole creative process. To the degree that the role is stilted, false, or unreal, I'm challenged as an actor to bring some kind of reality to it, and that's hard work. So, I would say that good material is much more stimulating to the creative process than mediocre material—no doubt about it. I'm also learning to determine good acting material more accurately on the written page. Movies are much more than the written words—so much sound and music and so many visual elements that aren't on the page—that the script sometimes isn't a very accurate guide to what the movie is going to be. But I'm getting better at divining what is there behind the words for my character. I've made some rather interesting mistakes by misjudging scripts in the past.

Do you have fun when you act?

It's getting to be more fun, a lot more fun. It can be terribly hard work on days when the energy's low, on days when the vital interest in the character, in the scene, in the relationships of this being, wanes a little. But, when it's cooking, it's really fun; it's exciting. It's the most exciting thing I can think of, actually.

In this book, I am exploring, amongst other topics, possibilities for change and transformation, assuming that we, as citizens of our culture, ought to change some of our habits or "act" differently. Do you think that some of the techniques that you use—your practices as an actor—are applicable to other areas, such as personal transformation?

For a person who is really serious about pursuing change, an actor's process can be very useful as part of the daily workout. I've never known anyone to merely say, "I want to be more loving" and then go about being more loving. It's a much more minutely detailed process than that, in my experience. The actor's craft in this process can be useful. A person could sit down in meditation in the morning, for instance, and say, "My relationships are distant and unfruitful. There are parts of myself in the foreground which are inhibiting the flow of love to my friends, and there's also something programmed in my multiplicity of personalities which is inhibiting the flow of my friends' love to me. Who are these aspects of myself who are afraid, who won't allow my vulnerable feelings to surface? Who are you? Speak! Now is your chance; speak to me!" And if you listen, they will speak. Using this process to become acquainted with disowned or troublesome parts of yourself is very useful. The first step toward change is not discipline but awareness.

160

Actors probably have an easier time with this process than non-actors because we are used to the process and we are not embarrassed by it. Your local bank manager is going to feel rather funny about sitting down with himself and saying, "Heart, speak to me!" But the fact is, his heart *will* speak to him. There's absolutely no doubt about it. But he must then listen.

Obviously, you are working with this yourself.

Oh yes. Not enough, but sometimes.

And you find success in doing it?

Definitely. I work formally with a gestalt therapist, both privately and in groups, as a kind of personal growth stimulant. It works! And every time I go to a group I see it work for other people too. Our feelings show authentically what we are in the moment. If we're in anger, that's what we are; we are anger. Most of us don't want to admit that. If we are envious, we don't want to admit it. And if we're loving, we're afraid to express it. That doesn't mean we have to rave like children about it, or be boorishly demanding of attention and unaware of other people's feelings. It means we must know from moment to moment what we are feeling and then choose how much to express and when to express with an awareness of the situation and the other people involved.

I read somewhere that your television specials, Thornbirds and Shogun, were two of the most watched in television history. How do you reconcile that very public identity of Richard Chamberlain with these very private, vulnerable things that you are talking of here?

Interesting question. I have no idea what the source of one's popularity is, not the vaguest idea. And I'm not sure I want to know. I mean I'm not sure that I dare ask the question; so I kind of ignore it and hope that I stay popular. Being popular brings work.

As to balancing the public person and the private person, that's a very tricky business. In *Doctor Kildare* I became very popular right away. Luckily, I was working long and hard. We started out doing thirty-six shows a year. The only times I ever got off the sound stage were to go on publicity trips or make quickie movies at MGM. So, for five years, I was pretty much in a kind of working jail, a terrific, wonderful prison of work that I loved. But I didn't have time to get big-headed about it, and I had some very perceptive friends at that time who, if I ever did put on airs, quickly put me back in place. There was also a part of me that knew my popularity as Doctor Kildare was a co-creation. It had to do with scripts, and with Raymond Massey, and with our producers and the other actors, all of whom created this mythical being who was not me, just part me.

But there is a shield that goes up when I go out in public; there's a shield up when I do an interview. (This is a different kind of interview—the shield is down pretty much.) But in a normal public relations interview, I'm very careful about what I say. I can't converse with a million people the way I can with an old friend. It's second nature to me now, putting up this public shield. I'm lucky in a way not to be a star of the magnitude of Robert Redford or Paul Newman—one of those almost archetypal beings who probably has to shield himself even more carefully against public demand, public need, public projection. Not that there is anything wrong with the public; the public's fine. It's just too immense a force to have to cope with when the shield is down.

When the inner dreams of Richard Chamberlain come out, what kind of world do you see? What compels you, not necessarily in your work, but in your life?

At the moment there are two long-term directions or paths that I can think of, and they're very hard to talk about. One is a non-intellectual, non-verbal need to experience life more deeply, whatever I'm doing, whether sitting here talking with you, or swimming, or reading, or acting, or whatever. I want to be less and less glib in my life, to be less and less general—more specific and more attentive to whatever is happening in the moment.

A related path that I can see is that of releasing myself from the motivation of fear. Fear gets more subtle as you get braver, but it's still there. It comes from a sense of separation from life, separation from other people. I would like to continue to move away from that sense of vulnerability toward a larger acceptance and awareness of the unity of life, the "alikeness" of human beings in all their individuality, and a deepening trust in the very essence of life, which I'm sure is the same in me, and you, and trees, and everything. Life is life.

We're taught, in this world, to fear, to feel separate, and maybe with good reason, because the process of finding our way back to wholeness is so fascinating and so illuminating. Maybe without fear in the beginning we would take everything for granted. So maybe it takes this struggle to make us really, truly appreciate what we're all about.

Are you ever concerned about the world's future, like nuclear issues or ecological issues?

I have different levels of thought about that. On a daily level, it frightens me that we are polluting our farmlands, and ruining our rivers, and threatening each other with bombs. Nobody seems to have a solution to anything, and our own economy and culture are so complicated now that things rarely work well. I was reading George Will's column in *Newsweek* the other day, and he was saying that, in current economic theory, everything is good *and* bad; everything is right *and* wrong; everything is productive *and* non-productive. He gave a lot of examples, and it's true. As Americans, we are living in a culture that is beyond understanding, but somehow we're muddling through . . . maybe. On another level, what is, is. There are all these cliches like: "There is nothing either good or bad but thinking makes it so." Perhaps it's true. Perhaps an atomic holocaust could serve some kind of cosmic purpose. I don't know; I know I don't want it to happen.

The only thing I personally can do is to find the balance within myself, not just try to focus on what I call "good" and eliminate what I call "bad," but to find the balance of light and dark, the balance of creativity and destruction. To find my own inner balance is the only real contribution that I can make to my culture and my society. And then, as that balance is found, to allow it to speak through my acting, allow it to speak through my political activity if there be any, through my presence. But to try to create peace out of chaos doesn't work. Each person has to find some way of balancing the inner chaos before speaking of peace.

What do you see as the new frontier of the arts? What speaks to you, and what do you think speaks to the world at large? What is relevant these days?

The power inherent in movies and television is limitless. I think certain filmmakers have occasionally gotten beneath the surface, have really begun to discover what's there. Art can do anything, can express anything, can touch us at any level we allow it to. I think artists will appear who can affect the audience as deeply as the audience wishes to be affected, and vice versa. The audience is a creative energy. Think what a movie is—artificial colors on a screen accompanied by mechanical sound. That's all it is. It's the audience that gives the movie reality and life.

I'd like to feel, as an actor, that I'm somehow involved in the evolution of my culture, involved in the whole process of our growth together, however messy that might be, however shocking that might be, however exalted that might be. We're all working together to find something out. It's a big, sometimes dirty, sometimes brilliant search; and it's tremendously exciting.

David Spangler is a writer, educator, and Co-founder of the Lorian Association. For twenty years he has addressed issues of personal and cultural transformation, the relationship of the personality to an innate sacredness, and the emergence of a "new age," a vision of the unfoldment of a spirit of synthesis and wholeness on the earth. Tapes of his lectures and his numerous publications have inspired and influenced the actions of many individuals and groups throughout the world. Mr. Spangler's books include *Revelation: The Birth of a New Age, Relationship and Identity, Reflections on the Christ*, and most recently, *Emergence: The Rebirth of the Sacred*.

David and I have been friends since our first meeting at the Findhorn Community in Scotland in 1971. At that time, he had already been established as a spokesperson for that community's philosophy and vision. David's unique gift is a clear inner vision which he is able to express in such a way that it empowers other people. In this interview, conducted in his home in October of 1984, I tried to bring to light David's process of giving verbal shape to those inner attunements, my assumption being that this process is an essential component of artistic work.

*   *   *

Mysticism is your art form. What do mystics do?

"Mysticism" probably means very different things to different people. It usually refers to something "otherworldly" and is most likely associated with a religious life of prayer and contemplation, meditation and retreat from the world. Usually the implication is that of someone operating on a different plane than the rest of us—not too relevant to the real world of earning a living or raising a family! Or sometimes the mystic is seen as someone special, a cut above the rest of us by way of a special relationship with God. I've known people who advertise themselves as mystics in the same manner as doctors or lawyers, as experts who the rest of us need to consult if we are to understand the spiritual side of life.

I feel both images are wrong. The true role and work of the mystic, as exemplified in the lives of the great mystics of history—such as Meister Eckhart or Saint Teresa—is not retreat, but a deeper involvement with life and a deeper understanding of its meaning and essence. To me, the work of a mystic is like that of a gardener, nourishing and bringing to flower the full vitality and spiritual power inherent in even the most ordinary aspects of daily life.

How does a mystic do this?

That depends on the individual circumstances and choices of his or her life. For me, it has been through writing and educational work. Because I'm married and have a child, it is also through family life. For another, it could be through business, science, politics, farming—any work can become a mystical activity. Whatever the outer form may be, though, the art of the mystic is to be a doorway through which we may see and experience, in an inspiring and empowering way, the presence of the sacred in our world and in our lives. The art of the mystic is to create epiphanies, moments when God breaks through the masks and disguises of our ordinary perceptions and becomes manifest. These are moments of joy and transfiguration, transforming our view of life and placing us more fully in touch with the wholeness that blesses and pervades creation.

A mystic works at this craft much as any artist. At best, he or she *is* the artwork. The mystic's life must be open to epiphany, open to the flow of the sacred. This means there is an inner component to the work, an inner journey to understand and contact the presence of the sacred, so that in the midst of daily life that presence can be recognized and affirmed. Yet, there must be an outer journey as well, a connectedness with everyday life and with the ordinary phenomena through which God manifests. As in any artistic endeavor, the flow must be complete from inner to outer, from inspiration to manifestation.

But, although these epiphanies, these moments of contact with the sacred, can be the most powerful events in our lives, they are not necessarily marked by powerful physical or psychic phenomena. They can, and usually do, manifest in simplicity, which is why they are so often overlooked. An artist can create an impact with just a few simple lines and sketches; he does not need always to use a large canvas and every color of the rainbow. Similarly, the work of creating epiphanies—epiphanogenesis, to coin a word—is neither always obvious or grandiose. So, the work of the mystic is to enable us to see and recognize that epiphanous nature of our lives and world by constantly seeing and recognizing it for himself or herself. It is the art of embodying a perspective or, to use my earlier image, of being a doorway through which the rest of us can see what might otherwise have been missed. And through that seeing, we can become mystics ourselves.

Can you say something about your own mystical experiences?

From my earliest memories as a child, I have had an awareness that there is more to life than what we see around us physically. Sometimes this awareness has been heightened by two kinds of experiences. One is a direct perception of the inner worlds through a sense that seems to be a combination of seeing, hearing, and touching, all blended into one sensation. It is an active sense, rather than a passive one, in that I must extend myself in some fashion and contribute to the act of perception in order to experience something more than just a background awareness. I use the metaphor of a bat's or dolphin's sonar: something must go out from me and interact with the inner worlds before I get a clear response. That response, in turn, acts upon my own capacity to form mental images. It is this power of imagination that allows the translation of the response into forms I can understand and interact with.

So imagination is an important part of this experience.

Absolutely. We commonly think of imagination as making things up, a tool of fantasy. But every creative person knows that imagination is the foundation for everything in our human world; it is the starting place. Something is imagined and then brought into manifestation; we live in a world of concretized imagination. Furthermore, what we call imagination is really part of an inner organ of perception. Even on the physical level this is true. What we see about us is not what is really there; we see images created in our minds—images of chairs, trees, houses, birds, and so forth—that emerge in response to electrochemical impulses in our nervous systems.

You mentioned a second kind of experience as well. . . .

Yes. This is the experience of an essential presence or quality in creation. For me, it is the experience of God or of the sacred; it is the classic mystical experience. This experience has taken different forms in my life, but whatever the form, its basic nature is unchanged: it is the merging with a presence that is the essence of love, joy, life, light, and the power of unfoldment.

How do these two types of experience interrelate?

The experience of the sacred is the most important to me. It has always been the inspiration for my work in education, allowing me to share my insights in ways that allow others to experience the sacred in themselves and their lives. And it enables me to use my inner sense in a more skillful manner, so that I can better project the qualities of love and wholeness. It also gives perspective to the experience of the inner worlds, which is, after all, only a perception of a class of phenomena. It's easy to become attached to phenomena, whether physical or psychic; attention and attunement to the reality *behind* all phenomena is a way of avoiding that.

Could you elaborate on what you mean by "the inner worlds?"

Consider the electromagnetic spectrum. The part of it we see, the visible spectrum, is really very small. Without some kind of assistance, we see only a tiny fraction of the "life spectrum," of which physical existence is only a small part. Metaphorically, it is divided into wavelengths just as the electromagnetic spectrum is. The physical world we know is only one such wavelength, and there are others which I call "the inner worlds." Some of these other wavelengths are very different from ours and have little or no connection with us, except in the sense that everything in creation is connected. Others are very connected, overlapping with our world, like the realm of the angels or of the nature spirits that the Findhorn Community in Scotland contacted. There are realms whose primary function is to provide an overarching structure of protection and guidance for the earth, to provide the matrix and inspiration for our further development as a species and as a planet.

You have gained a reputation by conversing with the "upstairs" beings who inhabit these inner levels. How does this take place?

I do this using the inner sense I've already described. I project my own energy of attunement to God—you might call this a form of prayer—and focus it toward a particular wavelength of service, one of those realms whose function is the care and development of humanity. I receive a resonance in return, patterns and configurations of meaning—I suppose they could be called symbols, but they are actually a unique sensation for which there is no direct physical analogue. It is a little like those experiences in dreams, in which you are both an observer and a participant in events, functioning from several points of view at once. I then begin to translate what I am seeing and experiencing into words and images of a more finite and human nature. I imagine this process is similar to that of a painter translating an inspiration into specific images and languages of color and technique. What I experience, however, are not images; I translate them into images to gain focus.

Could you give an example of this?

They are like living plays, little scenarios that I both observe and enter into. When watching a film or a play, for example, mental and emotional responses are triggered, some of which are directly related to the subject matter on the screen or stage, and some of which are not. However, the whole experience is a gestalt, a wholeness, and it has meaning for you. In an analogous way, I both observe and participate in a scenario which has its own content and which gives birth to related content, all of which comes together in a multi-layered experience of meaning, perception, and insight. This takes place very quickly, often in a matter of seconds or minutes. Again, as in a dream, the most complex adventures seem to cover hours and days, but have actually transpired in only a minute or two. Time, as we know it, is not really a factor in this inner experience. What does take time is the translation of the experience into a form others can assimilate. To continue my analogy, it is like coming home from a movie and trying to tell someone else what the experience was like, not just the content and plot of the film, but also its various nuances—its impact on you, and so forth—for all those things contribute to the meaning of the experience.

Would you describe a scenario?

It depends on the question someone may ask or on what I am attuned to at a particular time. For example, some years back, I experienced a configuration that, to me, meant there would be an accident at a nuclear power plant. I watched this pattern begin to move toward manifestation over a period of months and observed that some of its energy was taken away, that the configuration changed. In my own way, I worked with this pattern through prayer and meditation so that it would not manifest as I had originally perceived it. Finally, the pattern did embody as the accident at Three Mile Island, which we now know was far worse than was originally reported. However, if the original scenario had manifested fully, it would have been an even greater disaster.

This experience illustrates some key points: that human consciousness is interactive with these patterns in the inner worlds, that they can be changed through our actions, thoughts, and prayers; that the correct interpretation is not always what I might think it to be; and that timing is a factor that is difficult to pinpoint exactly.

Are your experiences generally prophetic, then?

No, most are not. Most of the things I tune into are patterns concerning what I would call cosmological issues: the meaning of life, the nature of the soul, the evolution of humanity, theological matters, and so forth. These are the things I lecture and write about.

Part of your art is to interpret those images in such a way that the tone is still alive even when translated into the rather restricted form of language. You experience something that is really very elusive, and you make those elusive impulses conscious for yourself and for other people. It seems that on an inner level you see a film, a process, and when you speak, it comes out as a slide, a statement. How do you bring an impulse into form so that the richness of the process is not lost?

There is no question that something is lost, just as telling another person about a film cannot fully replicate your personal experience of it. There's a good phrase for that: "You had to be there!" The way I deal with this is to be very aware of the loss, so that I do not take with absolute seriousness, nor allow others to take too seriously, the images that come up as part of the translation process. In other words, one must be playful; one must play with the process while being as deliberate and precise as possible. I am continually translating the slide back into the film, to use your metaphor. And I try to help others realize that the meaning of the slide comes not from the picture presented by the slide alone, but from the film as a whole. I encourage people to find the film within themselves, using the slide I give them as a starting place. When the slide takes on greater importance than the film, distortions come in and problems begin. Unfortunately, many people prefer the slide because it is static, and they can hold onto it, while the film is dynamic, a process that can be threatening because it is constantly changing, and evolving, and demanding that we evolve too.

Do you think that the relationship with the archetypal level, the level that you relate to, is available to everyone?

Yes, I do.

So, what you are experiencing is not unusual?

No, though the *way* I experience it is probably unique to me. But I do not feel the experience is by any means unusual.

Is there an imperative for you to express and communicate those images to others?

Only in the sense that an artist feels a desire or an imperative to share his creativity and vision. It is not a messianic imperative or a feeling that I have a message the world needs, except as it speaks to the positive nature of our future. It is lighter, more playful than that for me. I feel so blessed and vitalized by my experiences of the presence of God's love and by my sense of the positive future that love can help us to bring about, that I want others to share it with me. Occasionally, I have a prophetic insight, a precognitive experience about specific events; but mostly what I tune into is an awareness of the power, the love, the protection, and the caring that is made available to humanity. We have immense problems, but we also have an immeasurable source of guidance to resolve them and transform our society into something better than we have ever known.

So you have an unconditional trust and faith, a knowing, that the end result of all this human suffering and faltering is good?

Yes. It will lead to an incarnation of the sacred in our world.

You are well-known for your writings and teachings on the birth of a new age. What do you mean by a "new age?"

To me, the new age means a time in history when we will adopt different attitudes about ourselves and our world that will allow our perception and our expression to be more holistic. However, it also means a state of mind, one that is open to the spiritual qualities of breakthrough, of transformation and birth, and of creativity. It is a deeper understanding and experience of the power of the sacred that Jesus talked about when he said he would make all things new. There is a spiritual presence available to us that honors the past but is not bound to it; instead it always opens us to the ever-new, ever-renewing and creative spirit of God. It is one of my deepest spiritual experiences that this presence is very active in our world and is being born in us—in all humanity—in a new way.

Can you describe this new presence in human history? What are its components and attributes, and what are some of the ways you see it being absorbed into our consciousness?

I think it is being absorbed mostly unconsciously, in part because we do not as yet have a language to talk about it. I would call it an impulse for synthesis, for a deeper understanding and embodiment of connectedness on our planet. Our developing ecological sensitivity is the beginning of such a language, and it should also contain an element of what I would call the "otherworldly," connecting us to what is beyond our earthly experience.

Does that include space travel?

That is part of it. The space program, like ecology, is part of a language that helps us gain perspective—a way of looking at our world and ourselves in a much larger context. Similarly, what would a Galaxy-centered spirituality be? Most of our spirituality is anthropomorphic, rooted in the human experience, particularly in our Western culture. A new spiritual impulse might challenge those definitions and expand them to incorporate other perspectives, helping us to appreciate the non-human face of God.

Suppose we met an alien race that in no fashion looked like us, that might have ways of behaving that we do not recognize as being intelligent, and we wanted to establish communication with them. How could we do that if we are put off by their non-humanness? What spirituality might bring us into a deeper pattern of mutuality and sharing? This is the same question we face in dealing with our various ecological crises. Because nature is non-human, we often treat it in very unspiritual, unwholesome ways. Now we must change that attitude. So one element of this new spirituality would be that which helps us move beyond our current definition of humanness.

I would like to pursue the issue of language. You mentioned that space travel and ecology can be seen as languages that transform perspectives and thus consciousness.

In a sense, life itself is that language. A language is not only the innate structure and capacity to communicate, but also our ability to perceive it as a langauge. For example, the space program provides us with an image of the Earth from space, which offers a

whole new understanding of where and who we are. We begin to see
our world in terms of its organic nature, its fragility, and its
importance. That challenges other perceptions and languages of
separatism and enmity. The language of our divisions becomes
challenged by a language of planetary perspective and unity.

*It seems to me that we are victims of our language. Though
language is an extension of our thoughts, it works the other way
also, and thoughts become extensions of language. Part of the
challenge today is to develop new languages in order to begin to
think differently. What are some other new languages? Are there
any in the arts, for example?*

Art in our time may need to become more participatory. What Naj
Wikoff did with the Prairie Ship, or what you were doing back in
Yugoslavia, draws people into the artistic endeavor. The holistic
planetary perspective is one of participation; so any act that fosters
a participatory language contributes to that perspective. Also,
participation heightens our perception of *ourselves* as the embodiment of our art, rather than thinking of art as something to hang on
a wall or put in a gallery. That would mean a heightening of our
individuality and of our engagement in community, the two
modes—private and public—through which we manifest. Participatory art would seem very important in leading to that possibility.

Then, too, the definition of an artist changes. I see the bioshelters
which John and Nancy Todd and the New Alchemists have developed, for example, as artistic representations of the world we live
in—miniaturizations of ecology—which put the world into a form
we can observe but which also demands participation. A bioshelter
is a living, dynamic entity; without participation, it ceases to be a
bioshelter. The same is true for the earth; that is what ecology is all
about. This is art in a planetary sense.

So, one of the characteristics of this trend toward a planetary
culture is the participation of the individual. The collective does not
participate; it is not an organ of experience. There is no such thing
as the "American" perception; there are only the perceptions of
millions of Americans, which in many cases do not coincide. The
ability to perceive and be involved rests with the individual. If I
participate in such a way that it cuts off the participation of others,
if I diminish the ability of others to participate, to make choices, to
perceive, to think, to be sensitive, then I destroy a participatory

culture at its roots. To me, the totalitarian condition, in whatever framework—family, group, nation—has, as its primary character- istic, the deadening of the ability of its members to participate.

Democracy by name can be totalitarian in function.

That's right, because it can lack the larger context of connected- ness. The new culture that seeks to emerge has this paradoxical function of enhancing individuals' performances, always in rela- tionship to honoring and enhancing the performance of the whole. In that sense, the art of the recent past, in which the artist is so wrapped up in subjectivity, does not prefigure this new culture. Such art becomes a rather selfish statement; the artist as celebrity defeats the possibility of the artist as celebrant. It is the individual as celebrant that is needed in the new art.

What do you mean by "celebrant?"

For example, a priest performing a mass is a celebrant. But a priest is not doing it for himself alone; the intent is to have the entire congregation caught up in the experience of sharing the mystical body of Christ.

So the celebrant is a passage through which power moves. What about you as celebrant?

I've come to a point where the language of expression that I have been using—speaking and writing—feels limiting to me. In some respects the lecture circuit, and the "new age" field in general, is becoming too celebrity-oriented for my taste. I want to take time off from my public work in order to freshen my inspiration and explore some other options for communicating my ideas.

Any insights as to what those might be?

Perhaps children's stories, fiction, films, games—things that are fun. I'm interested in the power of play to teach and to transform.

When I started lecturing twenty years ago, I probably would have defined myself as a prophet—someone who spoke out of an ongoing series of inner revelations, inner experiences, without trying to integrate "the stuff" for people; I gave them raw material and let

175

them do with it what they wanted. Then, in my book, *Revelation*, which is a series of prophetic statements, I started to explain things in an attempt to help people integrate the information. But an artist does not always explain; let other people do the explaining, and you can do wild and crazy things. A prophet is like that; I think that the sacred is like that. Part of my need now is to go back to being wild and crazy again. I have gone as far as I can in trying to explain things, and I want to go back to my prophetic side. After all, by human standards, God is wild and crazy. Faith is wild and crazy. Love is often wild and crazy. Art is wild and crazy. If we remove all the wildness and craziness from our lives, we will die of unrelieved logic and the loss of inspiration and innovation. I'd like to be able to integrate those wild and crazy things into a new language.

But there is a difference between a prophet and a wild man: though the prophet might do and say things that, on the surface, seem strange, he is still deeply integrated in the cultural process. He carries a healing and nourishing connection to the well-being of the whole. I have known very few prophets. But there are a lot of crazy mystics, psychics, and sensitives who give out what they perceive without integration and cohesiveness. That is born of a selfish vision; it is only noise, not a true message.

In that sense, we could say that art must move from wild to prophetic statements, and artists themselves must come to terms with their inspirations and their wildness.

It seems that what blocks the transition from wildness to prophecy is the self, the ego. An artist can become so much the perfected technician that he may need time to go back and touch some of the prophetic and revelatory domains. Behind every good artist is a wild statement, the presence of a wild vision that is almost impossible to incarnate. For some, that creates a sense of hopelessness. But, for me, it is just a knowing that, amidst the things of this world, there is a spirit that can hardly be expressed and can never fully be captured in words or forms. Therefore, however much we strive to do so, we cannot exhaust that spirit nor come to the end of the wonders and mysteries that it will always have in store for us.

Ellen Burstyn

Ellen Burstyn is a distinguished actress of stage and film. In 1975, she won the Tony Award for Best Actress for her role in the play, *Same Time, Next Year*, and the Oscar, Golden Globe, and British Academy Award for Best Actress for her performance in *Alice Doesn't Live Here Anymore*. Her other film credits include *Tropic of Cancer*, *The Last Picture Show*, and *Resurrection*. Ms. Burstyn is a five-time nominee for an Academy Award, as well as the recipient of a Drama Desk Award, Outer Critics Circle Award, two Golden Globe Awards, the New York Film Critcs Award, and the National Film Critics Award. In 1982, Ms. Burstyn was elected to a three-year term as President of Actors' Equity Association. She is also the Artistic Director of the Actors Studio and serves on two panels for the National Endowment for the Arts. She is a lecturer and writer and holds two Doctoral degrees: Dr. of Humane Letters from Dowling College and Dr. of Fine Arts from the School of Visual Arts.

I first witnessed the immense skill and power of Ellen's work in the film Resurrection, *in which she portrays a woman who finds within herself the gift of healing. After an introduction by a mutual friend, she very graciously consented to participate in this book. In June of 1984, I stopped by her home north of New York City. There is an extraordinary beech tree in her yard that I have come to love and, after paying our respects to this ancient friend, Ellen began the following conversation:*

*   *   *

When I act, I go through a certain process that is unbearably painful, in that it touches very vulnerable places. I do that consciously by performing every night, but when I talk about it, the experiences get de-charged, which depletes my work. I would hate to talk about it to the point of losing its magnetic force for me. Do you understand what I mean?

I do, and I appreciate it. Can you explain what you mean by "painful?"

It's sort of probing, reaching around and isolating the feelings that are recorded inside, touching them and releasing them again. In other words, your life and your experiences become the notes of the instrument that you play.

Are you saying that you can only perform a role that touches experiences in your own life?

No, because it is not a literal experience. If a character I am playing experiences awe, for example, then I look in myself for a time when I experienced awe, recalling all of my sensory memories of awe. That's what Lee Strasberg taught; he called it "sense memory." So, if I wanted to recapture this day five years from now, I would probably start with the temperature, feeling the heat of this day, and the river, and how it looked, and the song from that little bird out there, and the feel of these clothes on my body. The more sensory levels of reality I could bring in, the more of this day would return. If this day also had an emotional content, in rebuilding all of this sensory stuff, the emotional experience would come back. It's called "affective" memory.

So, in that sense, acting is very real.

It is; when it's right, it's real. When it's pretending, then it's something else.

Is it possible that a person who is not a professional actor can apply this same reconstruction method? For example, we all have special moments of being connected with the world more deeply. If we want to be in that mode more often, can we just reconstruct it?

Sure. One of the most profound experiences I had was on top of the mountains in the Alps, in a camp facing Mount Blanc, one of the most beautiful places in the world. I was there only three days when I got a message that my son had been thrown from a horse, and I had to go to him. I suddenly felt reluctance to leave. I wandered off by myself, sat on the edge of the mountain facing Mount Blanc, closed my eyes, and said something like, "Oh mountain, you are so beautiful, and I find myself unable to leave. What should I do?" And the mountain said, "Take me with you!" So now that mountain is available to me anytime in my life; if I'm in agitated circumstances, I can re-form the mountain in front of me. I think that's a type of meditation, don't you?

Yes, I do. So, for you, this principle works not only in acting, but in your daily living.

That's right. Also, a character may have certain experiences that I haven't worked on; she may be working through something that I haven't been able to work through in life. By her working through it, I then learn that lesson in my life.

Maybe when people say an actor or an actress has depth, they are seeing a depth that comes from the courage to be real in life. It is a paradox that suggests that acting is very real.

That's what I always say to young actors. Most people think that acting is pretending, but it's not true. In life we build up social masks; when we act, we lift them. So people really go to the movies to see people stop acting.

In one of our previous discussions you made connections between acting and priestly work. Can you say anything more about that?

Well, there's not an awful lot known about what went on in the first temples. In that period there were priests and priestesses who enacted what were called the Mysteries. The Mysteries then were probably the same as the mysteries now: life, death, birth, transformation, regeneration. People came to these temples to see the Mysteries enacted. It's very hard to recognize my own faults, but it's very easy for me to recognize yours, right? And when I see them in you and become annoyed, it's usually because they have something to do with me. Well, through the Mysteries, people understood themselves better because they saw reflections of themselves.

It's the same with movies. I don't know if the big event of a movie is seeing the movie or the conversation afterwards: "What did you like? Did you like him? Did you like her? I didn't like her. I liked him. Well, I'm not sure—I didn't believe her; I believed him. I thought he was funny." Everybody comes away with an opinion. There's some kind of unraveling of a movie—taking it apart, finding what worked, what didn't. People go to the movies and then check out what was presented against their own scripts, the scripts of their lives. And they tally, or they don't.

I'm wondering to what degree you pull this image of enacting a mystery—the priestly function—into your current work?

Well, I don't think of myself as a priestess. I do question, when I do a movie, what I am representing—what mystery, what archetype, what human dilemma, or what issue I am addressing. And the issue can be sociological, psychological, political, or mystical; it can be on any level.

Not having been brought up in this country, I am not familiar with all of your work but, in what I have seen, there seems to be a consistency in your choices: a very articulate and conscious upholding of certain values, and ideas, and qualities. What are the criteria by which you choose your scripts?

Well, they change. Sometimes life is very cooperative in allowing me to make the best choices for my career, and other times, life has other lessons to teach and suggests that perhaps I will do a film whether or not it's the best career move I could think of making. "To thine own self be true." It's hard to explain what that means for me.

Do you have any regrets about some of your choices?

Well, whether or not I'd make some of those choices now really isn't the issue. I always put everything through the same process of examination. What comes up "yes" once might come up "no" another time. But for that time it was "yes," and you can't have regrets. You *can* have regrets, as a matter of fact, but you can't sanction your regrets; you can't encourage your regrets. Somebody introduced me the other night by saying that I'd won an Academy Award for a picture she had turned down. It happens all the time in the business that there are parts that people consider their parts, that they didn't do, that you did, or vice versa. You just have to let go of that. That's my form of Buddhism; it's how I practice non-attachment—letting go of anything from the past that throws up regret.

Do you ever find that in real life you invoke a character that you have played and shove that character in front, because it might be easier in the moment?

Only if I'm playing with it; only if it's fun to do. It is as if there are many different voices inside, and I am the accumulation of all those voices. I can move all of my energy into one voice, into one space, and relate from that one voice inside of me, broadcasting it into the world, bringing it back in and taking it to another place. I don't think that I exploit my ability to do that.

In fact, one thing that I find very disturbing about the process of acting—in the way I feel is the right way to do the work, which is with full vulnerability—is that it makes me more vulnerable. People expect actresses or actors to be able to appear in public more easily than other people, but it's absolutely untrue. When I appear, when I face an audience directly, when I don't have the mask of the character, then I feel totally exposed and so uneasy, and much more nervous. I feel like all my skin is off, and I'm just nerve ends showing. The work is a sensitizing process. In that way acting relates to the enactment of the Mysteries, because the training is a sort of ritual sacrifice; it's a feeling of peeled skin.

It seems to me that one of the qualities of good acting is having empathy for people who are different from yourself.

There's an element of every person in each of us: all possibilities are in each of us. So it's a matter of isolating a possibility, moving into that space, and speaking from there.

What happens after you end a film or play? Do you need a decompression chamber?

Yes, I have to refocus the energy. Many really fine actors have difficulty closing down their energy after a performance. They're flying, and they have a couple of drinks to pull themselves down. I find the drive from the theater to my home—which is about thirty minutes of being by myself—very useful. And the home atmosphere pulls me down. It's interesting to me what acting energy is. For instance, I use a different acting energy for film than I do for stage.

Being true to your character in filmmaking must be more difficult, I imagine, because the flow of work is broken down into short scenes, while in a stage performance there is a continuum.

And the presence of a thousand people adds so much energy. It's not just the energy that you give off; it's the energy that you take *in* from all of those people. There is an exchange between actor and audience, so the actor leaves the stage charged with the energy of everyone in the theater.

It's like a ritual in that sense.

Yes, because it's a coming together. It's similar to the role of priests and priestesses of the old cults, because a play focuses the energy of the group, of the gathering.

And the quality of the focus determines the quality of the ritual.

And vice versa. The quality of the ritual also influences the quality of attention. For instance, in a superb performance—like the one Dustin Hoffman is giving now in *Death of a Salesman*—when the actor is at a peak, the audience is in perfect harmony. All of their attention is focused on one spot—just like in a meditative experience—and I'm sure that they're all breathing together.

Which is the purpose of ritual—to unite people.

That's right!

But to unite people without diminishing their individuality. . . . Hitler was a supreme ritualist.

It's transformation of energy, and Hitler transformed people's energy into a destructive force. He literally fed off their energy. In the presence of a great performance there is a "glimpse of the Godhead." The glimpse of the Godhead comes in moments when the energy is being transformed, when the audience and actor come together. The energy goes right up to the peak.

How often does it happen in your work that you feel the ritual of your acting has been successful?

Well, I've just done a play at the Manhattan Theatre Club. It's always my intention to have that happen at least once a night. Sometimes it does, and sometimes it doesn't. I played for six weeks, eight performances a week, and I would say there were maybe four nights that it did not happen. But I have done whole plays where it did not happen. During the production of *The Three Sisters*, it didn't happen because I did not connect with the character in a proper way. I couldn't find the way into her, or I couldn't find her in myself. It's not that I can't; it's that I didn't then.

Was that your personal observation, or did other people, like the critics, notice that lack of connection also?

I don't know. I didn't read the reviews, but I think they were not very good, judging by the look on my friends' faces. But I'll do that part again sometime, somewhere else, and connect with it. It was then, at that time, under those circumstances, that I couldn't make the connection.

To what degree does a good director facilitate that connection?

The performance is supported by the entire company, and the set, and the music, and the lights. A director brings all that into being, hopefully. Some directors don't; yet it all comes together anyhow, in some synchronistic way.

Do you find this transmission of energy happening in any of your colleagues? For example, when I interviewed Richard Chamberlain, he mentioned Sam Shephard, whose picture I see there on your wall. Did you have that experience when you worked with him in Resurrection?

183

I think the thing that sets Sam apart from all others—not only actors, but people in general—is his amazing intelligence. I don't think he has more talent; I think he has more mind, more intelligence. He's very, very conscious.

Conscious of what's going on in himself or in the world?

He's very in the moment, conscious in the moment. He'd made only one picture before we worked together and he hadn't yet developed techniques for acting; he hadn't developed the tools. But his intelligence was so enormous, and his creative imagination was so enormous, that what he couldn't do, what he wasn't able to achieve technically, he could accomplish with such intelligence that it didn't matter. Just his being in the moment, knowing what he wanted to do and knowing when he hadn't achieved it, was powerful. That really is what star quality is.

It's such an interesting phrase, "star quality." What does it mean? Through "stars" there's a glimpse of the Godhead. Buckminster Fuller used to talk about stargazing, and he said that all of the thoughts of the greatest philosophers traveled out and bumped into stars, and then traveled back to us. So when we're stargazing, we're reaching out there, and great ideas come to us from bouncing off stars. It's the same thing that happens with stars on the silver screen.

You're one of those, aren't you?

I don't think of myself that way. I suppose I think of myself as a craftsperson, like a potter. Mel Gibson has that quality in *The Year of Living Dangerously*. And Linda Hunt is just so spectacular! All the time I watched her I was not only enjoying the movie, but was also being a professional actress looking at another actress' technique. There were moments when the transformation was so powerful that she *was* a man.

Speaking of transformation. . . . There are many thinkers who claim that a transformation is occurring in our time which affects the way we inhabit the Earth and live with one another. To what degree do these issues occupy your thoughts?

Well, my feeling is that we are bringing in a new age; we are giving birth to a new age. I see a huge difference in the world around me from, say, twenty years ago, and not just in all the frightening ways. I see people relating much differently, for instance. The manifestation of androgeny around me is startling—I see more and more people who are balanced in their masculinity and femininity. It's like a lining up of the male and the female energy in each person. I see relationships that are very different. And women have gone through an incredible transformation.

"We are bringing in a new age." Who do you mean by "we?"

Whoever wants to, whoever does, whoever will put in the work, and the energy, and the time, and the concentration. To me it's a day to day thing. It has to do with being honest in some mysterious fashion; it has to do with being real and going back to your own inner voice and asking, "Is this the right thing to do?" I know the right thing to do if I really listen inside.

It seems to me that things are getting better. The Hudson River became polluted, and now it's getting better; it's being cleaned up. As the pressure has intensified over the last century—certainly the last decade—things have gotten more and more intolerable. People who are sensitive to it—artists, healers, psychics—have been feeling this intensification of energy, and now there's a release, an exhaling, an expressing. I felt for a couple of years that I didn't have anything to express; I felt I was going through a long inhale. And now I am starting a long exhale.

What do you think is trying to be exhaled?

I think balance is one of the key words, and reconciliation—with the soil and with the planet. It's a balancing of forces; we're entering a time of integration. The Earth is becoming healthier, and I feel that people are relating with more consciousness of spirit than they did in, say, the '50's. Remember the *Time* magazine cover story in 1958—I think it was entitled "Is God Dead?" It seemed there was a great low point of spiritual energy then, or of spiritual awareness. Now in the '80's, it seems there's an integration of all aspects of ourselves—our physical, mental, emotional, spiritual, and cosmic selves. A very balanced time—that's what it feels like to me.

Do you sense that balance in your own life? Are the changes you talk about reflected in your life?

Yes, in events as they happen. Like the big tree last year, which suddenly had scale on it. A bug was eating the leaves, and we were trying to decide whether to spray or not to spray. We decided not to, and as we sat out there with it, all of a sudden a huge swarm of birds came and started circling the tree, and they just went round, and round, and round, and ate all the bugs, and cleaned it off. We watched and marveled at this. It was like the tree was vacuum-cleaned by a little cleaning squad sent down from the sky. When I witness events like that, it makes me not worry.

There is a process at work in our lives that I am acutely aware of and completely mystified by. On the day that Martin Luther King was assassinated, my clock radio woke me up with Doctor King's voice saying: "I am not afraid. I've been to the mountain; I've seen the other side. And my eyes have seen the Glory of the Coming of the Lord." And I sat straight up in my bed and said: "Doctor King will be assassinated today." I told my husband I had a vision that King would be shot during the march. We went to the beach and stayed there all day. Suddenly I said: "We have to get to the radio—they've shot Doctor King." We turned on the car radio and the announcer said that Martin Luther King had just been assassinated.

Nobody can talk me out of that experience. It happened. And I have no idea in the world how. There are voices in my head that speak to me, that guide me. I'd like to know who's on the other end of that line? Who am I talking to? How did they get my number? I would like to understand the process by which that kind of knowing occurs. Things like that, of course, happen on a much less dramatic scale, and sometimes I notice them. But I do not understand them. And it is curious that we are made that way, that we have these potentialities that we tap into once in a while, experiencing a different reality. Why not all the time?

Marko Pogačnik

Marko Pogačnik, a Yugoslavian artist, sculptor, teacher, and writer, was one of the founders of the OHO group, an association of young artists whose works have been exhibited throughout Europe. Over the past six years he was commissioned to create a series of public monuments, including a network of twelve monuments in Vipava Valley in Slovenia, Yugoslavia. Of primary importance to Marko has been the recognition of forces within the Earth and our relationship to them in the way we build. With this in mind, he has published guides to various cities—Vipava, Novi Pazar, and Venice—focusing on the harmony between those forces and their integration into art, architecture, and urban design. In 1985 he co-authored with William Bloom *Leylines and Ecology: an Introduction*, published in Great Britain.

Marko and I have been friends for twenty years, and though we have lived on two different continents for half of that time, seeing each other perhaps every three years, we have made parallel discoveries concerning the need for the artistic spirit in our time. I have always admired his deep attunement to the land and his powerful artistic language. The last time I saw him was in March, 1985, when we visited together most of his public monuments in Vipava Valley. In Marko's view, his monuments function as conductors of energy, and I have found that to be true. I asked him to write an article about his growth as an artist, and he sent the following.

*   *   *

During the spring of 1962 I felt a strong desire to detach myself from the superficial materialism that seemed to govern my social environment. A love was born within me for freedom of expression, and I was inspired to shape my own style of thinking and communicating intimate truths. Prior to that time of inspiration, I had understood art to be merely a cultural ritual, conforming itself to life as it is. Afterward, I knew art could be a source of power, able to confront and renew the disintegrating world. It was then that I published my first poems and exhibited drawings and ready-made sculptures. But my artwork proved to be too challenging for the cultural administrators who had, it seemed, adopted a very narrow definition of artistic expression in the style of social realism. As a result, I experienced a great deal of political pressure, and soon realized that inspiration was not meant to be a force of confrontation.

I then began to better understand the complexity of art with its emotional, mental, energetic, and material dimensions. Coupled with the artist's capacity to reach beyond the limits of the "known," art represents a multidimensional space within which new ideas can manifest, much like the delicate phases of growth a child experiences in the security of its mother's womb. Within a maternal space created by art, a new culture can safely evolve before being born into everyday reality, exposed to the pressures of a rigidly structured world.

Between 1966 and 1970 I worked with a group of friends, including Milenko Matanović, to develop an embryonic culture which we called the "OHO" movement. OHO is an artificially created word, a bridge between OKO (in Slovenian meaning "eye") and UHO (meaning "ear"). It connotes the intermediary position of artwork, which is not attached to the spiritual or aural world of vibrations nor to the material, visible world. We felt that art should open toward both sides of reality. We envisioned a kind of a-humanism, understanding humanism to be a breakthrough during the Renaissance, freeing Europe from the bonds of religious consciousness that had developed during the Middle Ages. Such a break may have been necessary at that time, but during the following centuries, human self-centeredness evolved beyond completion to the limits of self-destruction which we face today. How could we be humanists after that?

So instead, we discovered art as an instrument of listening, awakening to the vibration of different worlds without destroying their autonomous organisms. We became aware that while we stare at things, those things also stare back at us. The hierarchical way of thinking, with humans at the top, gave way to a dialogue between multiple worlds, different life-forms, beings belonging to various evolutions.

An installation from my exhibition in the Belgrade Palace of Youth in 1969 is an example of this idea. Metal weights of different values were fastened upon white rubber belts which stretched due to the force of gravity. There was no trace of any artistic hand. The gravitational pull—or the love of the Earth that is attracting everything upon the planet toward its center, as I would perhaps call it today—showed itself through the sensitive relationships between the particles of matter, the weights, and the force working upon them directly. I felt that an artist's work should not pierce the foreground, but should instead facilitate from within the possibility that beauty and truth would be directly apparent to the spectator.

The third phase of work coming out of that initial inspiration brought me to the countryside of Šempas, Slovenia, where I live with my wife and three children. During the intense years of the "Šempas family," from 1971 to 1979, I became absorbed with the task of building a balanced life, where animals, plants, minerals, human beings, and cosmic forces could exist together in mutual respect and cooperation. We discovered the beauty of the Art of Life and, for me, art as an activity separate from the rest of my life ceased to exist.

This seemed at first to be the ideal model for the art of the future. When art exists everywhere it has an invisible presence: the original

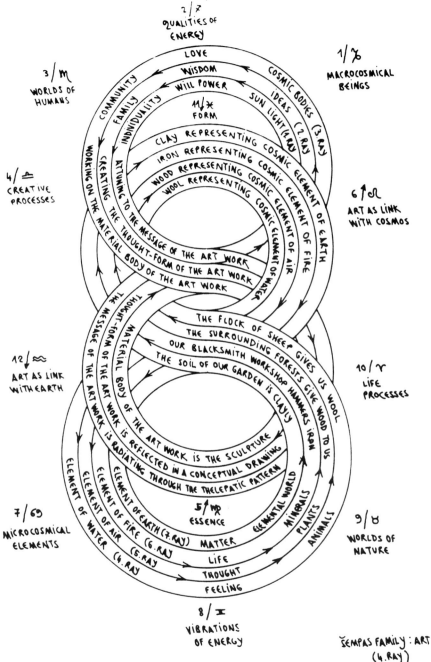

Diagram representing Marko's life-as-art orientaton.

literature is hidden in the way we talk to each other; the primeval architecture is contained in the way we design our homes. It is certainly not what art is today: literature frozen into linear book shape; architecture as an extension of technology; sculpture exhibited in galleries, separated from the mainstream of life. But the concept of the Art of Life showed itself eventually to be a polarity. As long as the art lived, all was well. But when we were invited to communicate the essence of our work to the wider public, we discovered that it could not be demonstrated without transforming our family life into a kind of "theater." More and more people were coming to our place, inspired by our example, to find support for their own searchings. Our intimate family life was constantly disturbed, and our children were pushed aside in the constant demand for our full attention by the public.

In this dramatic situation we discovered artistic language again. Thus, from "life-as-art," art as a specific expression of life was reborn. We began to build sculptures made of four elements: wool, wood, clay, and iron. We had a flock of sheep which gave daily milk and provided the wool that was used as binding material. Similarly, we used the clay from the earth, iron from our blacksmith workshop, and wood from the surrounding forest. Thus, the materials of the artwork were a direct expression of our daily life. Yet there still existed a trace of separation between art and life. On one hand, the art was lived, and on the other hand, the life was expressed through the art. Could the two be joined in synthesis? Could the artwork also perform a service to the social and natural life of its surroundings?

A form of answer came to me in 1979, when the village community of nearby Vrtovin asked me to build a monument there honoring the thirty villagers who, as partisans, had sacrificed their lives during the Second World War. I held open meetings with the village people to jointly formulate the concept for the monument. We discovered that a pyramid-shaped mountain peak, which ranged above the village, was a significant part of their landscape, and they wanted a link to be made between the mountain peak and the monument.

I was able to feel the life-force that came down the slope of this peculiar mountain, nurturing the life in the valley; we had obviously identified an etheric energy line. I decided that the elements of the future monument should be arranged in alignment with this line of energy. The idea was that the monument would become a permanent tool, capturing this energy and transforming it into mental and emotional patterns which could be absorbed by the community.

Vrtovin Monument, created in 1979 with the assistance of the villagers. Made of stones from houses destroyed in an earthquake.

During the following years I was invited to build a dozen such monuments which I call "landscape sculptures." The first element in my working process is always to listen to the specific radiation of the chosen spot on which the work should be built. Intuitively, I try to envision the patterns of energy moving through the earth and atmosphere of that fraction of landscape. When I am working with a village or town, I try in my imagination to remove the artificial urban

192

structures in order to start a dialogue with the internal energy patterns of the place.

As we know, our planet is alive because of the network of high frequency energy lines permeating its body. We call them "ley-lines." The Chinese call them "dragon lines." Especially important to the unique character of a place are minor lines of energy called "aquastats." They come into being where the magnetic power of a major line, or ley-line, interacts with the material structure of the Earth, water, or air. Their courses, often playfully shaped, are constant, and represent the invisible "liquid" counterpart to the visible but "frozen" form of the landscape. Ideally, the arrangement of the stones, the images cut into them, and the layout of the paths within the structure of a monument can physically reveal the invisible energy patterns already existing in the location.

I work with peasants and have discovered that they have a deep sense of the secret life of the Earth and the specific type of energy that characterizes their particular place. They may speak in stories or make "silly" suggestions, but it is my task to detect the underlying message. I also try to find ways to include the craftsmanship of the local people in the actual process of building the monument. In this

Sculpture of the Four Seasons, created in 1983 at the University of Ljubljana. Materials are recycled railway ties.

193

way they are given the chance to co-create the artwork, which builds links to the social environment as well.

There is another element in my working process which is not easy to explain. I have a notion that an artwork aligned with the Earth's energies becomes magnetized by them and creates an echo strong enough to vibrate on levels of beingness higher than our own which we could call "cosmic." I believe that, on those subtler levels, the message and shape of an artwork are being complemented and co-created. Perhaps these complementary overtones are what the Greeks referred to as Muses! I seek attunement to this invisible part of the process by asking questions inwardly, like children do outwardly when seeking answers from their parents.

I see modern art narrowing to its own end, step by step, by becoming less relevant, more ego-centric, and more exclusive. It will ultimately die, at which point art can be reincarnated in daily life in a new and higher quality. For me it is important to be aware that artwork in material form represents only part of a broader artistic process which operates simultaneously on different levels of time and space.

Milenko Matanović

Milenko Matanović is an educator, lecturer, musician, and
artist. He majored in Art History at the University of Ljubljana in
Yugoslavia and, along with Marko Pogačnik, he was one of the
founders of the OHO group, an association of young artists whose
works have been exhibited throughout Europe. Between 1975
and 1983, Milenko and his wife, Kathi, have given concerts
throughout the United States, Canada, and Great Britain and have
recorded several albums of original folk songs. Their latest album,
Cycles, was released in 1982. As an educator, Milenko focuses on
the themes of transformation, specifically the roles of spirituality
and the arts in cultural change. He is a Director and Co-founder of
the Lorian Association and a founding Director of the ETA
Project.

195

*I met Suzanne Duroux at a meeting of ETA Project Associates in
August of 1984. She had been doing research on the issue of the
role of art in social transformation for a Master's thesis and
requested an interview with me on that topic. We have since
become associates, working closely on the various programs of the
ETA Project. In putting this book together, she convinced me to
include that interview as a more personal expression of my work
than what was presented in the introduction.*

*　　　*　　　*

What was your motivation in founding the ETA Project?

I am interested in projects that enhance the importance of artistic
vision and integrate that vision in our culture. The ETA Project
addresses these issues by looking at the creative processes at large
and, specifically, at the arts. The assumption is that artists synthe-
size an inner awareness with outer crafting, producing forms
which, at their best, resonate with the environment and enhance
life. I see a direct connection between artistic awareness and the
needs of our culture.

Can you explain that further?

In my mind, after our basic survival needs are met, what rises for
us is the need for a "home," an environment that invites belonging,
within which such intangible qualities as beauty, love, and communion can exist. If we are made in the image and likeness of God, I
would say that it is a God who is a supreme artist and creator of
wonderful things—universes, galaxies, stars, planets, mountains,
oceans, fish, bugs, and people—and that we must learn how to
create with a similar imagination and sense of beauty and a deeper
awareness of our connection with all life, not just human life. So
now, since our notion of "home" has expanded to embrace the whole
planet, I suggest that the earth can be our ultimate art project.

There's a gift that artists can give to our time that is much more
than making pretty objects. It's the gift of understanding the
process of creation, the end result of which is the world of forms, of
the things that we make and build—economic structures, social
structures, and cities. So I ask, "How are we as ordinary citizens
aware of that image of ourselves? Are we exercising artistry in our
lives? Are we good artists?" These questions are especially pertinent

in current times: the wake of destruction that often follows our actions indicates that we are *not* good artists in our daily lives. Either we have a distorted image of what human beings are all about—an image fostered by our inflated sense of superiority over the natural world—or we have just not mastered our crafts well enough. But we are vandals, laying the earth to waste and leaving behind an industrial graffiti that cannot be erased.

So, if I speculate about changes for our world, one possible future is a culture where artistic sentiments flourish, not only in museums and the homes of the wealthy, but in everything we touch. We could create beautiful houses, and beautiful cities, and beautiful roads, and beautiful businesses. Now, I know the notion of "beautiful" is up for discussion, but by it I mean things that are more resonant with our inherent needs for connectedness.

What is your background as an artist.

In one form or another I have practiced the arts throughout my life: drawing pictures as a boy, playing violin, singing folk songs with an all-male choir in Yugoslavia, and later composing my own songs, performing and recording them with my wife Kathi. In my late teens, I worked as an experimental visual artist, focusing on alternative languages by which the arts could communicate with society. I experimented with artistic works in the fields, forests, and rivers. In one work, for example, I tied white wooden sticks together with string—creating a fifty-yard long snake—and placed it on the surface of the river. It curved with the bends and currents of the water and made the beautiful meanderings that always existed there more obvious. The art was not in the value and craftsmanship of the materials, but in the idea. I wanted to make my fellow citizens more aware of the subtle beauty existing at all times around them.

At some point during that progression away from making artistic objects toward creating awareness, I became mindful of the power of my perception. I realized that the *way* I see conditions *what* I see. One day I wakened and saw everything as I had never seen it before. Perhaps I suffered from temporary amnesia! In any case, I was amazed by the richness of what I saw: the details, the textures, the colors, the people. I realized how easily I had projected familiarity onto the environment out of laziness, perceiving only what I had already concluded to be true and, in the process, denying the world ever to be new.

Since then, I have tried to be aware of the filters and biases through which I look at my world. It is not that I wish to disown them; I simply want to be aware of their existence and become strong enough internally to let go of them. Henri Matisse said, "To see itself is a creative operation, requiring an effort. Everything that we see in our daily life is more or less distorted by acquired habits, and this is perhaps more evident in an age like ours when the cinema, posters, and magazines present us every day with a flood of ready-made images which are to the eye what prejudice is to the mind. The effort needed to see things without distortion takes something very much like courage."[1] I think that it *does* take courage to see the world for what it is.

Does this mean that you are discouraged about the state the world is in?

No, I'm optimistic, which does not mean that I do not forsee a lot of challenges. I see the immediate future as a series of planetary vaccinations: disasters will happen which will be big enough to teach us lessons, yet small enough that they will not be catastrophic. And I trust our capacity to learn from our mistakes. One does not need to be very insightful in order to see that our mistakes are now confronting us with an unconditional and awesome ultimatum. But this obviousness can be the gift of our era: in the shadow of ecological deterioration we can see clearly the unintegrated and destructive side of human creativity. And when we see this shadow, we can deal with it—if we own up to it.

So, if we truly "own up" to what we do on the earth, we need to acknowledge that whatever comes about will not be a surprise; we will have created it. How can artists help us to shape our intentions?

Our current cultural makeup prioritizes certain options and neglects others. One modern priority is efficiency—time is money—and what is of value in that mind-set are things that are done as quickly as possible. We have not, however, asked ourselves about the consequences of these doings—whether or not the world benefits from our notion of efficiency. Is efficiency an ultimate good? Our industrial makeup is very "masculine" in that way; it's inspired by outward motion rather than inner communion.

As James Hubbell has pointed out, artists are like raw nerves; they deal with the issues with more intensity, perhaps because they are more affectable, more sensitive. Artists can respond to the issues that confront us culturally and take them to a deeper level of consciousness, where the challenge is not polarized, but is resolved internally. Works that come from such a transmutation do not simply mirror or magnify the challenges, but demonstrate the solution. This is a very private process that can sometimes be lonely. One begins with an exasperating speck of dust, but can end up with a beautiful pearl.

So, one of the contributions artists can make is to take issues upon themselves and find an inner correspondence to the outer problems. Even the nuclear issue can be a very private one: it is a symbol of unintegrated energy, of misapplied power and creativity. It is a ghost, by which I mean that it is a force that has lost its touchpoint with human reality and has, like a disembodied soul, nowhere to go. Each of us can either contribute to the power of this ghost or diminish it through integrative actions.

Isn't that a painful process as well, insofar as we identify with the archetypal image of the suffering artist?

I do not think the issue is pain or no pain, but rather honesty and a willingness to be open to what surrounds us. There are moments of discomfort and emptiness in everyone's life. For me, those moments come around in cyclic fashion. At times I have dealt with them awkwardly, trying to sidestep them. But over the years I have come to cherish them, to listen to the silence and emptiness. In most cases they offer new ways of looking at the issues I am dealing with or bring new elements into my working equation. At best, those moments are times of revelation. So now, when I experience discomfort or pain, I try to stop and listen to what is behind it. I do not want to be blind to pain; I want to take it in without surrendering to it and see if I can turn it into a gift.

It wouldn't be very helpful to the world if the message from artists was that, in order to create a healthier planet and good lives for ourselves, we need to be in pain.

Right. But where there is pain—and there *is* a lot of pain in our world—we can transmute it, turn it around, through our questioning and embracing it, rather than running away from it. There are artists—good artists—who are mirroring the fragmentation around us, and either we have these painful reflections or, at the other extreme, a happy and popular art that bypasses the challenging issues. I'm looking for some kind of synthesis of these two approaches, a way to respond with honesty and integrity, taking things in and returning small, personal solutions which can add up to a great force.

Are you involved in any projects that incorporate this sort of solution?

I have an idea for a project that I would like to bring about sometime soon. It combines ecological reclamation with planetary consciousness and the arts. In the Yugoslav part of the Adriatic Sea there is a chain of islands called Kornati, which was devastated by a giant forest fire a century or so ago, leaving the islands bare and rocky. John Todd explains a desert reforestation module in his interview, a technology that would make our planet green again in twenty-five years. That boggles the mind! His work is wonderful fertilizer for my imagination. My fantasy is to take one of those islands in Yugoslavia and, over the course of twenty years, bring it back into lushness. Then a sanctuary or a special open space in honor of the Sacred Earth could be built there, and pathways could be traced over the energy lines, following geomantic principles. The result would be an island that could function as an artwork, nourishing spirit, nature, and human hope. The "chapel" could be filled with artworks from around the world. I would ask the Yugoslav government to dedicate the island as an independent territory, belonging to the planet and linked with other such places on the earth. Each would be like a mini-earth of the future: a most wonderful green and beautiful place where people could rejuvenate themselves, and go deeper into themselves, and appreciate all that is good about the human race. Each could become a place of celebration of the spirit and nature.

Another project that we are developing through the ETA Project is called *City as an Artwork*. I feel privileged to have grown up in the city of Ljubljana, which is now visited regularly by city planners and students of architecture from all over Europe. The city is one of the clear examples of good urban planning undertaken in the early decades of this century by Jože Plečnik, a brilliantly sensitive architect. I only now realize how much the early experiences of my native city and traditional village life influenced me in my attitude toward city living. I was aware of Ljubljana as a living entity which, like any organism, finds its maximum health when all of its natural and human traditions are integrated. Romans referred to that as the "genius loci," meaning the "spirit of the place," which gives life to people and places and determines their character and essence. It is like an underlying pattern or language that, once understood and experienced, can guide people's choices. Architecturally, that translates into patterns that weave human functions together with the existing terrain.

Ljubljana, for example, grew around a "spine" between two dominant hills. Several years ago that spine was severed by the building of a new highway, and it was very interesting to hear from friends there how strongly the impact of that action was felt by them. It was as though the whole city had a headache. It made me wonder to what degree all actions, both sensitive and insensitive, impact our living. Look at the way we design our cities around cars instead of around people. Cars are an efficient way to get us from point "A" to point "B," but how many neighborhoods have been destroyed by running highways through them? Or, in going to see the beautiful things in a museum or gallery, we often have to go through a lot of ugliness to get there—the parking lots, noisy streets, air and noise pollution. We feel it's okay to segregate art into a special department and not let it live outside; we have art zoos. I think that our lives are impoverished as a result.

So, "City as an Artwork" is designed to enhance the realization that cities, too, are vital organisms, each with a unique spirit, and to integrate artistic and ecological sensibilities into the decision-making processes that affect the patterns of a city's growth. It is a series of events designed to release the imagination and creativity of a city's citizens. For example, school children might visit the elderly residents of various neighborhoods in a city and ask them about the changes they've seen over the past decades—their joys over the gains or griefs over the losses—and use the stories as raw material for artistic projects in the schools. Or, artists might be commissioned to occupy places at key locations throughout a city, and citizens would have the opportunity to work with any of these artists to create images or stories drawn from their own ideas about their city's future. The artists would work in the manner of police artists who create portraits from descriptions.

These are only two ingredients of a model that we are developing, a model that uses artistic imagination as a way to integrate sensibilities which are often neglected, yet are vital for our well-being. Walking, for example, is such an essential function for humans— meeting and looking one another in the eyes, not passing each other like non-entities as we do from our cars. Isn't that what creates a human community? The simple things. And we've created many urban environments where that simple function cannot be performed anymore. The design of many of our cities discourages connections with other people and with the land. So I suggest that the artistic process can be an example of working in a way which does not damage things in order to create, but is mindful and sensitive to what is in the environment—natural or human— sensitive to the *true* needs of people rather than the invented ones, drawing all the elements into a higher resolution, a higher synthesis. Great art always does that; it's only lousy art that destroys something in the process.

Is that how you personally determine the value of an artwork?

My basic definition of art is this: the creation of forms that invite connectedness. Good art connects me with other people's stories, with the cultural or natural environment, with the unknown. Good art seems to be created with gratitude and thankfulness. Poets, for example, are as thankful for the language and its words as for the ideas they desire to express.

I think that, as citizens of a modern culture, we would do well to reintegrate the sensibilities and craftsmanship of some pre-modern peoples. When Native Americans killed a buffalo, they used every part of the animal's body. Prior to the killing there would be a prayer that in effect said: "My brother Buffalo, I'll kill you, but not out of hate. I'll kill you because that's how the world works: you eat grass, and I eat you, and we're all part of the Great Spirit." So crafting, in that sense, is the art of creating something new without spiritually destroying what preceded it. The Native American might say, "Because I make a drum out of your hide and make you into a teepee, and because I eat you with thankfulness, and because your bones are going to be used as tools, you will continue to live through my gratitude, my brother Buffalo." That's thankfulness. The same attitude could hold for those who cut down trees for buildings: "I'll use this wood to make a house, but you, dear tree, will continue to live through my appreciation. You will live in my memory." One of my favorite examples is the sensitivity with which traditional Scandinavian builders went about building their homes: they created a clearing in the forest and the trunks of the trees they cut became the main pillars for the dwelling. The trunks were positioned in the identical way they grew naturally, for they believed that the spirit of the tree would continue to live in the wood and benevolently influence the house.

And, of course, we consider those things to be superstitious now—the spirit of animals or trees—I mean, who still thinks or talks about spirits in nature? Such an attitude is considered downright pagan. But when you think about it, it's a powerful image of how to create with nature. If we, with our awesome might and tools to manipulate, approach our work with thankfulness and respect, wouldn't we create a world that leaves less destruction in its wake? This is "applied" art; it's integrated into everyday existence and is every person's responsibility. When that responsibility is exercised, choices such as how to build roads, or parking lots, or cities tend to reflect a collective artistry. The Balinese, for example, have no word for "art" because art is so integral to living that there is no need to give it a special name. They simply do everything as well as they possibly can, integrating the perception and value of beauty into the mainstream. Or in Japan, simple activities like the tea ceremony or the art of flower arrangement incorporate artistic sensibilities. Or in Italy, artistic excellence has had a powerful tradition which some feel has been central to it's tremendous economic success over the past three decades.

So your early environment was a powerful influence on your work. What were some of the other influences?

I have also been influenced by what I call "holy" moments in my life, moments that stand out in my personal horizon above everything else and help me orient myself in my choices. To respond to those moments has been my spiritual practice. Now I should point out that, for me, spirituality and religion are two different things. Religion is participation in a belief that someone else has created; spirituality, on the other hand, is based on one's own experiences, which can be identical to those of other people and influenced by clear examples, but the starting point is trust in one's own perception. Spirituality emerges from simple and direct experiences that bypass images and language and has little to do with ideologies, beliefs, or cosmologies. There are no "shoulds" or "should nots" that come from those experiences, but simply an unconditional and compelling power to draw us into deeper participation with life. I have had experiences of both ecstacy and pain, when something broke through into my consciousness with such power that I *knew* it was telling me something important. I have come to trust those moments; some of them will last me a lifetime.

Would you describe one?

I had a dream a year or so ago in which I saw a person whose head was about to be cut off by a descending sword. Just before the sword reached the neck, the blade turned slowly to its flat side and descended onto the shoulders as in the ceremony of knighting. What had begun as an execution and death turned into an initiation. This dream suggested to me that the very same issues that confront us most can become—if we are willing to learn—sources of our initiation into a higher, more appropriate order. I think art is one of the forces that can help in that turning of the sword.

[1]*Henri Matisse: The Nature of Creative Activity, in Education and Art, ed. Edwin Ziegfeld (New York: UNESCO, 1953), p21.*

THE ETA PROJECT, a division of The Lorian Association, was initiated by Milenko Matanović in 1982 in the belief that the arts offer a significant contribution to the process of cultural transformation. The purpose of the ETA Project is to explore, demonstrate, and communicate the unique role of the arts in inspiring individual and collective transformation; to imagine and formulate possible futures; and to foster excellence and artistry in all areas of our lives. For more information about the ETA Project and the work of Milenko Matanović contact: The ETA Project, P.O. Box 663, Issaquah, WA 98027.

THE LORIAN ASSOCIATION is a non-profit educational corporation established in 1974. It provides, through its research and public programs, a spritual, philosophical, and practical vision of an emerging planetary condition alive to the possibilities for increased harmony between all peoples and between humanity and nature.

LORIAN PRESS is the publishing division of The Lorian Association, producing materials which reflect the spirit and philosophy of Lorian. For a catalogue of publications write to: Lorian Press, P.O. Box 663, Issaquah, WA 98027.